HARD MEASURES

HOW AGGRESSIVE CIA ACTIONS AFTER 9/11 SAVED AMERICAN LIVES

JOSE A. RODRIGUEZ, JR.

WITH BILL HARLOW

THRESHOLD EDITIONS

New York   London   Toronto   Sydney   New Delhi

Threshold Editions
A Division of Simon & Schuster, Inc.
1230 Avenue of the Americas
New York, NY 10020

First Threshold Editions hardcover edition April 2012

THRESHOLD EDITIONS and colophon are trademarks of Simon & Schuster, Inc.

For information about special discounts for bulk purchases, please contact Simon & Schuster Special Sales at 1-866-506-1949 or business@simonandschuster.com.

The Simon & Schuster Speakers Bureau can bring authors to your live event. For more information or to book an event, contact the Simon & Schuster Speakers Bureau at 1-866-248-3049 or visit our website at www.simonspeakers.com.

Designed by Renata Di Biase

Manufactured in the United States of America

10 9 8 7 6 5 4 3 2 1

Library of Congress Cataloging-in-Publication Data

Rodriguez, Jose A., 1948–
  Hard measures / Jose Rodriguez ; with Bill Harlow.
      p. cm.
  1. Rodriguez, Jose A., 1948– 2. United States. Central Intelligence Agency—Officials and employees—Biography. 3. United States. DCI Counterterrorist Center. 4. Intelligence officers—United States—Biography. 5. Terrorism—United States—Prevention. I. Harlow, Bill, 1950– II. Title.
  JK468.I6R63   2012
  327.12730092—dc23
  [B]
                                                          2012003698

ISBN 978-1-4516-6347-1
ISBN 978-1-4516-6349-5 (ebook)

For the men and women of the CIA, whose skill, dedication, and selfless service have always inspired my admiration, loyalty, and awe

The author is donating a portion of his proceeds from this book to the CIA Officers Memorial Foundation, which was established in December 2001 to provide educational support to the children of CIA officers killed in the line of duty. For more information about the foundation please visit: www.ciamemorialfoundation.org.

CONTENTS

Preface

WHO I AM

I am Jose A. Rodriguez, Jr., the Puerto Rican–born son of two teachers. I grew up largely in South America and in the Caribbean, coming to the continental United States for the first time for any length of time when I attended the University of Florida, where I received my BA and law degree. For the next thirty-one years I served my country, undercover, as an officer of the Central Intelligence Agency.

After September 11, 2001, I was assigned to the CIA's Counterterrorist Center. There, I was responsible for helping develop and implement the Agency's techniques for capturing the world's most dangerous terrorists and collecting intelligence from them, including the use of highly controversial "enhanced interrogation techniques."

I am certain, beyond any doubt, that these techniques, approved by the highest levels of the U.S. government, certified as legal by the Department of Justice, and briefed to and supported by bipartisan leadership of congressional intelligence oversight committees, shielded the people of the United States from harm and led to the capture and killing of Usama bin Ladin.

What follows is the story of how my colleagues and I came to take those hard measures and why we are certain that our actions saved American lives.

HARD MEASURES

Chapter 1

RASHID RAUF

'm tired of you Americans saying we are not doing enough to fight the terrorists." General Ashfaq Kayani, director general of Pakistan's Inter-Services Intelligence, was polite but firm during the meeting at his home in Islamabad in August 2006. "We may soon have a chance to conduct a major operation—what I need to know is whether you are with us or not."

The confrontation was not the first and certainly not the last between his organization, the ISI, and mine, the CIA. As head of our National Clandestine Service, my mission was to oversee the running of covert operations, the recruitment of spies, and the theft of secrets on behalf of the United States. Since 9/11, the Pakistani intelligence service had arguably been our most important foreign relationship—but it never was or ever will be a smooth one.

Unbeknownst to me, and presumably to General Kayani, that sweltering August day in 2006, Usama bin Ladin and members of his family had recently taken refuge in a villa in Abbottabad, less than fifty miles northeast of where we sat.

We met in Kayani's home on a tightly guarded Pakistani military base. The residence resembled something you might see in an affluent American suburb. There were several parts to the structure, one for his living quarters, another section that appeared to be an office, and a third area where the general met visitors like me. He was casually dressed but all business. After subordinates served fruit juice and tea, Kayani let me know what was on his mind.

A casual eavesdropper on my conversation with General

Kayani might think, well, of course you would say yes to the general's request, and of course the U.S. and allied governments would applaud your action. But in the world of counterterrorism, nothing is straightforward.

The loyalties of the ISI will probably always be suspect from an American perspective. While some senior officers like General Kayani proclaimed their support for our counterterrorism efforts, others a couple of echelons below him were happily supporting al-Qa'ida and the Taliban, an organization that the ISI (with some U.S. help) had essentially created years earlier. How much ISI officers knew about Bin Ladin's whereabouts had always been hotly debated.

I had come to Pakistan along with the CIA's director, General Mike Hayden, in part to try to nurture the tricky relationship between the Agency and the ISI. After several days of meetings, Hayden returned to the United States, but I stayed behind to probe the state of relations between our two organizations. My concern was more than bureaucratic. We were in the midst of a looming crisis, one in a series of tense moments that regularly marked our relations with the ISI. I had spent the day flying around on a Russian-built Pakistani MI-17 helicopter visiting Peshawar, the Khyber Pass, and remote tribal areas where the CIA and ISI tried to work together against terrorist targets.

On my arrival back in Islamabad, CIA officers alerted me to some new intelligence that a terrorist cell in the U.K. that we and our British allies had been monitoring had selected specific transatlantic flights that they planned to bring down in an attack that would rival 9/11 in scale. *"Coño!"* I said to myself. There had been many chilling intelligence reports over the past five years, but the more I learned, the more this seemed to me the most concrete and imminent threat to the U.S. since the World Trade Towers were brought down. The near-unanimous concern about a second attack that had galvanized our nation in the days, weeks, and months following 9/11 had since abated among politicians, the media, and the general public, but those of us on point in the fight knew that the threat had not gone away.

In recent months, our British allies had learned of a U.K.-based terror cell and its plans to blow up as many as ten commercial airliners as they headed from Britain to New York, Washington, D.C., and California. Through excellent intelligence work, British intelligence and police officials had monitored plotters as they implemented an ingenious plan of draining soft drink bottles and replacing the contents with concentrated hydrogen peroxide and other chemicals, including the use of the powdered breakfast drink Tang as an explosive accelerant. The altered containers could easily pass through routine airport screenings that were in use at the time. Had they been detonated while all ten planes were at altitude over the Atlantic, there would have been a loss of life in the thousands. Evidence of exactly how the planes were brought down would have been lost at sea, and the panic in the international transportation arena would have been devastating.

The effort British authorities devoted to tracking the plotters in their country was extraordinary. It was said to be the largest domestic surveillance effort ever conducted in the U.K. There seemed to be nineteen potential suicide bombers involved. Coincidentally (or perhaps not), that was the exact number of people who carried out the hijackings on September 11, 2001.

The Brits originally learned of the plot by finding that one of the plotters had traveled from the U.K. to meet with a known al-Qa'ida operative in Pakistan.

The central figure in the plot was a man by the name of Rashid Rauf, a dual British/Pakistani national. The Brits knew a fair amount about him. Rauf was said to have been born in England of Pakistani parents and raised in the West Midlands city of Birmingham. He disappeared from the U.K. in 2002 in the middle of an investigation of the murder of his uncle. While never charged in that crime, he was definitely a "person of interest" to British authorities, not only for that matter, but also because of his known ties to violent Islamic militant groups in Pakistan. But they needed to know more about him.

As troublesome as U.S. relations with Pakistan can be, our British allies can have an even more difficult time getting full cooperation from the ISI. Hard feelings dating back more than six decades to the Raj when Britain ruled the region meant that often the U.S. was able to get cooperation from the Pakistanis in ways that eluded the Brits.

So the CIA took the lead in working with the ISI to try to track down Rauf and others in Pakistan who were behind the plot that was brewing in the U.K. Using our clandestine technical resources, we were able to determine that planning for the strike was coming from North Waziristan in the mountainous Federally Administered Tribal Areas of Pakistan.

The CIA approached the ISI to see if they could shed additional light on the whereabouts and plans of Rashid Rauf. Although the plotters in the U.K. were under intense surveillance, at the time we did not know the whereabouts of Rauf. During his visit to Pakistan, General Hayden let senior Pakistani officials know that we were very interested in him.

In my meeting with General Kayani a few days later I was told that the Pakistanis had learned that Rauf might soon be traveling from the tribal areas toward the city of Bahawalpur. General Kayani saw that there was a rare opportunity to roll up a terrorist and he asked me if the U.S. would support Rauf's immediate capture. I made an on-the-spot decision. "Absolutely. We want this bad guy!" It seemed to me that telling

Kayani anything else would have undermined the relationship we were trying to build with the ISI. I made the call despite a vague understanding that British authorities were hoping we would not move too rashly against Rauf. They wanted time to follow the trail of the U.K.-based terrorists to see what other leads might develop and to generate more court-admissible evidence for a future trial. But to me, the news that the plotters had moved to the point of selecting actual flights to bring down meant that we could not afford to wait.

When my meeting with General Kayani ended, I departed for a local hotel. Brigadier General Azmat Hayam Khan, one of Kayani's top subordinates and head of Pakistani counterterrorism, was supposed to host a dinner for me there as a way to build greater rapport with his senior officers. Such representational duties are among the more tedious of the chores of someone in my position, but necessary if you are hoping to maximize the support of your foreign counterparts.

The general was in the front seat of an armored sedan. Security vehicles led and trailed us as we wove our way through the teeming streets of Islamabad and headed for the hotel. In the backseat, I was joined by the CIA's chief of station in the region, whose name I am not at liberty to divulge. Within minutes, Azmat's cell phone rang. I could hear him fire off a series of urgent questions in Urdu. He turned to my colleague and said, "The plan, as General Kayani has said, is coming together. The terrorist Rauf is on a bus heading for one of our checkpoints. We want to proceed with his capture. Are you with us?"

My colleague turned to me. "What do you think, boss?"

"Let's get him," I said. The cautious thing would have been to consult with Washington. But doing so would have been the equivalent of saying "no." Washington never responds instantly—especially in a situation such as this where they would have wanted to have some meetings, develop position papers, do some contingency planning, and consult the British. But in my mind, this opportunity demanded an instant decision.

Scrapping the plan for dinner, our two sides, the CIA and the ISI, set up command centers to listen to live feed from our forces in Bahawalpur providing a blow-by-blow account of the takedown of Rashid Rauf. The capture, carried out by Pakistani troops with CIA officers providing high-tech assistance nearby, was almost uneventful. If only I could say that about the aftermath.

Once I was assured that Rauf was in Pakistani control, I called CIA headquarters in Virginia and told my chief of staff what had happened. I asked her to go down the hall and brief the deputy CIA director, Steve Kappes. She called back minutes later: "Steve is livid. He wants to know why you let the Pakistanis conduct the takedown."

"Because I agreed with them" was my simple answer.

She said that the Brits were insistent on following leads on this case a while longer to see who or what else might be implicated. "President Bush apparently told Prime Minister Blair a few hours earlier that we would move slowly on this plot," she said. My unilateral decision apparently had caused a diplomatic incident. Because of it, they were scrambling to arrest all the known cell members in Britain that very night.

I was sorry for any inconvenience to President Bush and Prime Minister Blair—although no one had bothered to tell me about their conversation beforehand. But I am convinced that the decision to capture Rauf was the right one. If you are operating in a place like Great Britain you can confidently expect that Scotland Yard can track a criminal subject clandestinely for weeks on end. But in a country like Pakistan, if a chance suddenly presents itself to capture someone known to be in the final stage of planning multiple, simultaneous terrorist attacks, you better take them down. You act immediately because the opportunity may not come again—and you may not get another chance before attacks are launched. If, in the wake of a second successful terrorist attack of 9/11 proportions, it were to be revealed that the head of the U.S. clandestine service passed up a chance to capture one of the plot's masterminds, the second-guessers outside, and especially inside, government would have been merciless, and rightly so.

As it turned out, the Brits were able to swiftly arrest twenty-five suspects. They eventually brought to trial seventeen on charges of plotting to commit murder. Three received life sentences. While the trials themselves may not be memorable to most Americans, the impact of the case behind them certainly is. It is because of this group that since 2006 you are unable to fly with more than three ounces of liquids in your carry-on luggage. Rauf's plotters' plan to mix commonly available chemicals in soda bottles would easily have killed thousands of innocent people in transatlantic flight.

The Pakistanis held Rauf in custody while the Brits rolled up the terror cells in England. Since Pakistan does not have an extradition treaty with the U.K., they refused to hand him over to the Brits and insisted that any questions we or the British had for Rauf be funneled through the ISI. Happy as we were to have Rauf off the streets, he was not under our control.

Three months after his capture, Pakistan moved to drop the terrorism charges against Rauf, allegedly for lack of evidence. They continued to hold him on explosives and false-identity counts, but in late 2007 he mysteriously "escaped" from Pakistani custody. He had been held at the high-security Adiala prison when his guards reportedly decided to allow him to go to a local mosque for prayers. Not surprisingly, Rauf did not return. Given the uncertain loyalties of some inside the

Pakistani security system, it is foolish to take for granted our ability to follow, detain, or interrogate terrorists using Pakistani surrogates.

Two years later, it was reported in the media that Rauf was killed in a U.S. drone strike. His supporters deny this fact to this day.

In the immediate aftermath of the arrest of the plotters in the U.K. there was a lot of finger-pointing. Unnamed British sources told the media that the U.S. had overreacted and brought down Rauf prematurely. My relations with British intelligence took a decidedly chilly turn. A bogus theory from American writer Ron Suskind received great play in the media, suggesting that President Bush and Vice President Cheney had ordered the arrest of Rauf and the establishment of the draconian "no liquids on planes" rules to somehow influence the upcoming U.S. midterm elections. This was a patently ludicrous assertion.

And in general, the media widely denigrated the takedown of the terror cell in the U.K., saying that some of the British plotters had not yet gotten passports or plane tickets and therefore there was no urgency, as if stopping a terrorist attack doesn't count unless the burning fuse is snuffed out seconds before an explosion. The pundits forget that if we had been so fortunate as to interdict any of the nineteen 9/11 hijackers months before the attacks they might have been dismissed as a laughable bunch of losers who didn't inspire fear or confidence.

The liquids plot saga turned out to be emblematic of my CIA career. If there was a common thread during my lengthy time at the Agency, it was that no good deed went unpunished. The liquid plot incident further drove home to me the importance of swift action, of nimble decision making, and of being able to hold and interrogate key terrorist suspects ourselves without relying on surrogates who have a different and uncertain agenda.

Throughout my career, controversy followed me around like a hungry dog. I wish all my decisions and all my actions were universally supported and applauded. But I am comfortable with who I am and what I have done.

I have been extraordinarily privileged to play a role in some historic events and believe I am uniquely positioned to explode some myths and clarify some mysteries that have heretofore gone unexplained.

As memories of 9/11 faded, political correctness and timidity grew. The unanimity of support that the intelligence community enjoyed eroded, and one by one the tools needed to fight those who wish to destroy our country have been taken away. Worse, those men and women who volunteered to carry out our nation's orders in combating al-Qa'ida found themselves second-guessed, investigated, and shunned.

It is doubtful whether the takedown of Rashid Rauf, which happened less than six years ago, could happen today. Certainly, the unilateral U.S. action that brought about Usama bin Ladin's greatly deserved demise, for all the good it did, also served to highlight the gulf that exists between U.S. goals and intentions and those of many in powerful positions in Pakistan.

General Kayani, who in 2006 was chief of the ISI, is now even more influential as chief of the Army Staff, one of the most powerful men in Pakistan. Given the embarrassment of UBL's being caught so close to the Pakistani capital, Kayani and his colleagues almost certainly would be less willing to join the U.S. in capturing a major terrorist on their soil. Knowing this, and also knowing that the United States has no strong options for interrogating and holding prisoners itself, if the U.S. could find another terror mastermind like Rauf, or even a successor to bin Ladin, we might simply be forced to eliminate him with a Hellfire missile rather than running the risks of attempting to capture him. The risks are not just to the lives of our forces but also to the fragile cooperation between our two nations. When terrorists are taken out by blunt force, our ability to exploit their phones, computers, and minds dies with them. The United States has chosen to unilaterally disarm itself in the war on terror; in writing this book, there is no more urgent message I want to convey.

Chapter 2

LATIN AMERICA DIVISION

Although I found myself deeply involved in the U.S. war against terrorists from 2001 until late 2007, my path to that position was an unusual one, to say the least. What follows is a very short synopsis of my first fifty years of life. I share this not because I think readers are anxious to know about every twist and turn in my formative years, but because the events of my first half century had a tremendous influence in shaping what happened during my tenure at the seniormost levels of the CIA.

My road to involvement in combating Middle Eastern and South Asian terrorism began in Latin America. No one would have pegged me as a future top U.S. intelligence officer when I was growing up. I am the Puerto Rican–born son of two teachers. Not long after my birth in the city of Mayaguez, my father, an agronomist, moved our family to Buga, Colombia, where he helped open an agricultural vocational school. Colombia was an unsettled place at the time; there was an insurgency going on that resulted in the massacre of tens of thousands of people across the country. One of my earliest memories was of our milkman allowing me to sit for a moment on the horse he used to make his deliveries. Years later my parents learned that the milkman was also a guerrilla and used his horse for things other than delivering milk, such as participating in the armed conflict.

After about five years, my parents took our small family (a brother and sister were born in Colombia) back to Puerto Rico. But a few years later my father took a job with the U.N. Educational, Scientific and Cultural Organization (UNESCO) and we returned to Colombia. Later he joined the Alliance for Progress, started during the Kennedy administration. After another brief stop in Puerto Rico we moved to Bolivia, where my father worked for the U.S. Agency for International Development (AID). While there, my father bought a horse and I was thrilled to take riding lessons after school from a young army captain by the name of Luis Garcia Meza. Nearly two decades later I would deal with him again. During my boyhood stay in Bolivia there was a coup d'état. The country's then-president was overthrown and I remember watching jet aircraft strafe La Paz. The Rodriguez family seemed to gravitate to where the action was.

In 1965 a revolution broke out in the Dominican Republic. President Johnson decided to send the Marines and the 82nd Airborne there to prevent the country from becoming a "second Cuba." But the American involvement was not all military. USAID directed my father to move there, along with his family, to help administer economic aid for the impoverished country. When we arrived in Santo Domingo the rebels were holed up downtown and the city was divided in two, separated by barbed wire with American troops manning checkpoints. There was a lot of fighting going on, particularly at night, and we got used to going to sleep with the sound of gunfire in the distance. I spent my high school years in Santo Domingo and established some lifelong friendships there. The people in the "DR" are among the most laid-back and fun-loving folks I have ever met. So I was shocked to learn that some of my high school friends' parents had been involved in the ambush that killed Dominican strongman General Rafael Trujillo just a few years before.

Although it may sound like a disorderly upbringing, I thoroughly enjoyed my youth. To me it was all about seeing new places, learning about different cultures, and experiencing the adventures that life in a foreign country offers. To my friends and neighbors growing up in Colombia, Bolivia, and the Dominican Republic, the Rodriguez family represented the United States. But we were emissaries from a country I barely knew. I had only infrequently been to the mainland U.S., mostly to visit an aunt who lived in Hollywood, Florida.

When it was time to go to college I decided to go to the University of Florida as an undergraduate with the idea of readying myself for a career in foreign relations. After completing my bachelor's degree with honors, I elected to stay in Gainesville and attend law school, not with the thought of practicing law, but with the notion that a law degree would enhance my chances of getting a job in national security or perhaps with an international aid organization such as the ones that employed my father.

Law school was tough. About a third of my classmates flunked out. Not without considerable effort, I graduated in 1974. A few months after graduation, I became intrigued by the idea of applying to the CIA. It sounded like the perfect answer to my dreams of world travel, adventure, and involvement in important matters. Shortly thereafter I received a cryptic phone call from a recruiter who had been advised of my interest. Without specifically saying where he was calling from, he told me that their "representative" would be in my area soon and would like to meet with me. That started a nearly two-year-long process of getting into the CIA.

I met with recruiters, took tests, flew to Washington for interviews with psychologists and case officers, and, on my third trip to D.C., took a polygraph test designed to judge my reliability and ensure that I wasn't already a spy—for someone else. I passed. The Agency amused me by insisting I take a Spanish language test before hiring me. They would have been wiser to insist on an English exam. I'm not sure how well I did on all the other written and psychological tests they gave me, but where I excelled was in the personal interviews. Two Agency officers from the Cuban operations group at CIA were among those who assessed me. I later learned that they went to bat for my candidacy, having been impressed with my "street smarts." Without their support I would not have been hired, because I did not fit the mold of the traditional career trainee recruit. This is a problem that persists in the Agency to this day.

While waiting for my application to be resolved, I went to San Juan and lived with my brother, who was working as a geologist. I supported myself by selling time shares and real estate, which turned out to be not only lucrative but also good experience for being an intelligence officer. Selling someone a time share is hard, not unlike trying to convince some foreign official to secretly work for the United States.

Eventually, in November 1976, I left Puerto Rico to fly to Washington and begin my career in the CIA. After a few months at the Agency headquarters, learning the language of intelligence and serving in some interim assignments, I was shipped off to "the Farm," the CIA's clandestine training facility a few hours away from headquarters. My class of new recruits included Cofer Black (who decades later would be my boss and then predecessor as chief of the CIA's Counterterrorism Center). Others from my class also rose to important positions in the CIA. Having gone through training under such unique circumstances, we developed strong bonds of comradeship, which lasted through our respective careers.

While at the Farm we learned the tradecraft of the clandestine service, how to spot, assess, and recruit foreign nationals to spy on behalf of the United States, how to conduct surveillance on others and avoid it for yourself, the use of disguise, how to drive like a madman to escape pursuit, and how to effectively use all manner of weapons and explosives when all else failed.

While the training sounds like fun, all of us trainees were anxious for it to be over so that we could go out into the field and actually DO the work we had trained for. Perhaps prophetically, the hardest part for me was not learning how to conduct operations, but learning how to keep headquarters informed of what we were doing. Each day after all of our training we would have to type up "intelligence reports" to our imaginary bosses in Langley about the day's take of intelligence. The many reports were typed on manual typewriters and each had its own specific format. For a hunt-and-peck typist like myself, that meant laboring away until 1:00 or 2:00 a.m. to complete the mission and being ready to go again by seven the next morning.

For your final exercise at the Farm you are sent out into an American city with a mission. You have to conduct surveillance of others, avoid it on yourself, and track down an elusive person. Using your guile and "tradecraft," you must get up close to him and make a "pitch" that he come work on behalf of the U.S. government. My team was sent to a large American city and I managed to sweet-talk myself past some restaurant employees with a credible cover story to gain access to our target. The person we were after had deliberately secluded himself to make it difficult for us to get to him, but our approach worked brilliantly.

My record at the Farm was good but not spectacular. The number one and two ranked trainees were women. I was somewhere in the middle of the pack. I rationalized that the Farm was like law school. The joke there was that the A students would go on to become judges, the B students would be good lawyers, and the C students would end up rich. At the CIA, some of the B and C students at the Farm ended up doing very well, because many had the interpersonal skills, the ability to think on their feet, and the good judgment to succeed.

• • •

Given my language skills, I was the first among my group to be deployed. Many of my classmates had to spend an additional year or more learning some new language. The government—being the government—decided that since I was a native-born Spanish speaker, it would send me to a country where another language is spoken. (Fortunately, I quickly became reasonably proficient in that language, too.)

I learned a lot about operations during my first tour and put to use the skills I learned at the Farm and elsewhere. At one point I befriended a local army ophthalmologist who happened to be treating the mother of the commanding officer of a cavalry unit. I told my friend of my love of riding, and before long I found myself invited to ride with the regiment. Shortly thereafter, a new president of the country took over who had once been in command of the same cavalry regiment. He continued to ride with them weekly. So there I was, one of the most junior officers, with daily access to the country's president. I can't report that I collected any earth-shattering intelligence, but I provided valuable insights to my supervisors. I remember a cable from headquarters arrived saying that according to very sensitive intelligence, the president was reported to be in ill health. I was able to draft an immediate response saying, "This officer went riding with him this morning. His cheeks were pink and he looked well while downing a cup of intense and very sweet local coffee."

I rode every morning with the president and his entourage, and every so often I would sneak out during the week for a ride in the afternoon. I called my horse "Business" so that I could legitimately tell my colleagues that I was "going out on Business."

While I did not try to recruit the country's president, I did accomplish the most successful recruitment of my thirty-one-year career during that tour of duty when I met my future wife, Patti.

A native of Massachusetts, Patti was teaching at the American school. I met her at a party at the Marine house at the Embassy and was instantly struck by her beauty and personal charm and warmth. A year later she left to go to graduate school back in Massachusetts, but I wouldn't let her escape for long. I went back to visit her and somehow convinced her to marry me just before being sent to my second duty station.

Patti and I got a house in that Andean country (which I cannot identify), and I soon found myself invited to go riding with yet another Latin American leader.

The president, who was an excellent equestrian, and his compatriots were engaged in jumping horses one day over some of the most challenging obstacles I had ever encountered. I overheard him say to one of his majors: "Let's see if the gringo has the *cojones* to do this jump." He slyly smiled and encouraged me to approach a particularly difficult fence. I had no choice. Fortunately, my mount did all the work, but, as a result of my horse's guts, I was soon an accepted confidant of the dictator. On another occasion, the president fell when his horse stumbled jumping over an adobe wall. He moaned and squealed in pain on the ground while one of his assistants rode back to the stables to get a car. I stayed with him until the car came back for him. He was taken to the hospital with a badly broken leg. He appreciated my help during the incident and invited me to join his Thursday afternoon rides, followed by a barbecue at the stables with his closest confidants, all cavalry officers. Because I was a bona fide horseman and spoke native Spanish, the group would often forget that I was an American official and that the U.S. government opposed the regime. They spoke frankly about what was going on and I paid close attention. It was very good for business!

We had no illusions about my riding companion. When I was back in the office doing my day job, I spent countless hours collecting intelligence about his malfeasance in office.

After a couple of years, I was surprised to receive a cable from headquarters telling me that I was to become the Agency's chief of station in a small Latin American country. Surprised, both because I was still a very junior officer and because I had to pull out a reference book to find where it was. (When I was in school, it had been known under a different name.) I was concerned when I read the State Department's "Post report," which made the capital sound like a dump. However, it turned out to be one of our favorite postings, due to the wonderful friends we made there, the laid-back lifestyle of the country, and the beauty of the country's barrier reefs. Patti went back home to Massachusetts to deliver our first son, Nicolas. Not long after he was born I got notice that my tour was being cut short and I was to be posted in El Salvador.

El Salvador was the most difficult overseas tour that we had. It was a country at war. The violence was pervasive, and many people died during the conflict, including a number of CIA officers, often as a result of airplane and helicopter crashes. We worried daily about our families and our colleagues. We had a stray bullet break the glass of the window in the room where my baby boy slept. We later found the bullet on the floor next to his crib. While I was driving home one day, the passenger window on my truck was shattered by a glancing bullet. We were all armed to the teeth. I always carried a 9mm Browning with me and had a sawed-off shotgun next to me in my truck. When I traveled up country in an H-1H helicopter, I would have an AR-15 semiautomatic rifle by my side.

I hardly saw my family during this tour because of the abundance of work. Four U.S. Marines had been killed in the Zona Rosa district of San Salvador and I dove right into the work of finding the killers upon my arrival at my post. A few months later the Salvadoran president's daughter was kidnapped, and we were directed to support the intelligence work in that case. We found her, but the government would not risk a commando operation to liberate her. While I was in El Salvador, a decision had been made to completely change the CIA's approach to fighting the insurgency. I had the responsibility of carrying out the new plan, something that was all consuming and difficult to do. Earthquakes, disease (Patti contracted hepatitis there), and violence were a way of life in El Salvador in the mideighties.

While we were in El Salvador, the country experienced a severe earthquake that killed about one thousand people. Patti, who was pregnant with our second son, was working as the Embassy's mental health coordinator when the earthquake struck. She had to crawl out of the chancery when the Embassy buckled under the force of the quake and was destroyed. Outside, the ambassador would not allow anyone to leave the Embassy compound due to the chaotic situation in the city. Back then there were no cell phones and our secure radio network went down, so there was no way to call in or out of the Embassy. Patti was very worried about our baby sleeping in our home, which was located on the side of a mountain. I was able to get home first and found our maid with the baby in the front yard of the house. A massive iron gate in front of the house had come down and a lot of things were broken inside, but the house suffered no major structural damage, which was not the case with many of our colleagues' homes in the American community. Patti was shaken by the tragedy and the two thousand aftershocks. She kept the baby by her side in our bedroom along with a packed suitcase and her passport in case she needed to make a quick exit.

While in El Salvador I had to deal with the death of a

young Agency officer who was killed in a helicopter crash. I got a call at 3:00 a.m. that one of our officers was missing and I had to coordinate efforts to send people out to find him. The accident happened around the time Patti was to deliver our second son, Alec, and I couldn't get back to Massachusetts in time for the birth. Years later when I was getting ready to retire from the CIA, I took Alec into the Agency headquarters lobby and showed him the star in the book of honor denoting agency officers lost in the line of duty. Pointing to a date in the book, I told him that that was why I was not present at his birth.

After more than a decade in the field, I was brought back to headquarters for my first Stateside assignment. I was made head of a branch of the Operations Directorate that focused on Panama and the Andean countries. Panama demanded most of my time. General Manuel Noriega was a thorn in America's side at the time. This was my first brush with Washington bureaucracy. I attended my first major interagency meetings with National Security Council, Department of Defense, and State Department officials and was stunned not only at how hard it was to get a decision made on anything, but also by how quickly anything important would leak to the press.

Although I was based in Langley, I was personally involved in running some of the more sensitive operations, because Panama was under close scrutiny by Noriega's security service.

One event about which I was particularly happy took place when Noriega was running a sham election designed to convince his countrymen that he had been popularly reelected. Using Panamanian expertise, the signals of major Panamanian radio stations were hijacked and accurate results from exit polls were delivered showing that Noriega was losing the election. It was a spectacularly successful operation and by late evening on Election Day Noriega was forced to stop the count and annul the election results. In doing so, he displayed his true colors, and it was the beginning of the end for his regime.

As the situation grew more tense in Panama, I came up with a plan that I thought was pretty clever—a covert operation that just might get Noriega out of office without bloodshed. Noriega was known to be a big believer in witchcraft, and he had a Brazilian witch doctor who had tremendous influence over him. So I conjured up a plan that made its way to CIA Director William Webster, proposing that we recruit Noriega's trusted witch doctor and put him on the Agency payroll. With proper handling of the agent, I hoped to be able to create circumstances where our witch doctor would tell the dictator that a nice retirement home in Spain was in his immediate future. Unfortunately, Judge Webster was not impressed, and he essentially cast me and my witch doctor plan out of his office. Instead, the United States followed a more traditional path: a military invasion that succeeded in removing the dictator but cost the lives of twenty-three U.S. troops and more than two hundred Panamanians. Noriega's retirement home for the next two decades would be a U.S. prison.

My next job took me back to the field and back to one of my boyhood homes. My parents were living in Puerto Rico at the time and I was happy to go nearby as chief of station. My tour was rather uneventful, however, with no revolutions or witch doctors to contend with.

After a couple of years I was plucked out to go to Panama to meet with U.S. Ambassador Dean Hinton, who was tough as nails and had a reputation of chewing up and spitting out advisors. It took me a while to win his confidence, but eventually I did so. The ambassador wanted me to work closely with the head of the military's U.S. Southern Command—first General George Joulwan and later General Barry McCaffrey. One of the challenges was dealing with the post-Noriega military environment. Members of the Panamanian army were transformed into police. Only the most senior Noriega army loyalists were cashiered. While there continued to be some security problems in Panama, they were manageable. The experience there stood in stark contrast to what was done in Iraq fourteen years later, where a political decision was made to disband the Iraqi army. That decision greatly contributed to the years of violence and unrest that ensued.

In 1994 I returned to Langley for my second full headquarters tour of duty. At first I was made deputy chief of Human Resources and later became deputy chief of the Agency's Crime and Narcotics Center (CNC). Working in CNC was an eye-opener for me. The Center was under the direction of the Agency's Intelligence Directorate, not the Directorate of Operations, under which I had spent virtually my entire career. In CNC, operations officers, also called "case officers," worked side by side with analysts skilled in targeting drug traffickers and international criminals. The traditional walls that separate the two main branches of the CIA were torn down in CNC, and I experienced the synergy of these disciplines working together. CNC also gave me my first significant experience in working with foreign partners outside Latin America. My duties took me to Thailand, Russia, and Eastern Europe. While on a trip to China, I got a call from my boss, Dave Carey, telling me that the then-DCI, John Deutch, wanted to make me chief of the Directorate of Operations' Latin America Division. For someone like me, who had spent most of his career in the Latin America Division, normally this would have been a dream come true. But the Agency was going through some extraordinarily turbulent times. Deutch had come into office intent on cleaning house in the Directorate of Operations. At the time there were multiple investigations by the inspector general that eventually led to the firing of two highly respected

LA Division officers. A few others were forced to retire and hire lawyers to defend themselves from criminal investigations resulting from the Iran-Contra imbroglio and covert operations relating to the Central American wars. It was my first experience dealing with the fallout from controversial policy decisions that were second-guessed and politicized when, years later, a different political party won the election. I learned some valuable lessons, which I used in the years following 9/11 to try to protect the people who worked for me.

The way Deutch treated these senior LA Division officers was a blow to morale throughout the Agency. Many Latin America Division officers were openly wearing black armbands around headquarters to visibly express solidarity with the cashiered officers.

Adding to morale problems in the LA Division was an order Deutch issued throughout the Agency directing a "scrub" of all our assets, the agents working on our behalf in foreign countries. Deutch wanted us to rid ourselves of sources whose hands were unclean and forbade officers in the field to recruit spies in the future who were "dirty" unless there was a special written exemption from headquarters. The net effect was a severe chill on potential recruiting of assets. Few officers in the field wanted to ask headquarters for an exemption and risk earning the disapproval of the politically correct Deutch. In my view, this "dirty assets" order had a negative effect on Agency operations around the world. Deutch's successor, George Tenet, reversed the order after 9/11.

I reluctantly accepted the offer to become chief of the LA Division. While I disapproved of many of the politically inspired decisions from higher management, I rationalized that if good people refuse to take on these kinds of assignments during times of struggle, the entire institution is only further weakened.

I wish I could tell you that I went to the LA Division and

restored its morale and effectiveness, but the truth is my tenure there was cut short. I was essentially fired from the position because of a very biased and unfair inspector general investigation, which I will write more about later. The IG's office is an important institution, but in my experience, both in the late nineties and after 9/11, it can have a damaging and corrosive impact on the Agency.

I didn't stay fired long. First I was temporarily placed in the security office, helping sort out a major personnel problem. In the wake of the scandal involving Aldrich Ames, a senior Agency officer belatedly discovered to have been spying for the Russians, there was a major effort at the CIA to step up reinvestigation of our officers. Many Agency personnel had trouble passing their polygraph exams. Whether they had done anything wrong was unclear, but they could not get over the polygraph hurdle. Under newly installed regulations, if an officer's case was unresolved after three attempts to pass the "poly," the case was automatically passed to the FBI for a criminal investigation. The FBI was in no hurry to resolve the cases, and the Agency felt unable to give the officers under scrutiny meaningful work. So we had scores of good officers who became what were known as "hall walkers," wandering around headquarters in limbo, never knowing if or when they would be cleared, or worse, accused of a crime they did not commit and frogmarched out of the headquarters in handcuffs.

George Tenet, who had just become DCI, brought in with him Ray Mislock, a former FBI special agent, to deal with security matters. I worked with Ray to try to bring some sanity to the security reinvestigation process. Eventually we were able to force the Bureau to bring some closure to the lives of unfortunate hall walkers.

My time in limbo, too, was about to come to an end. The IG hadn't hurt my reputation within the Directorate of

Operations, and I was offered a chance to go to Mexico City as chief of station. It would be the fourth station that I had led and possibly a nice way to top off my career.

Our stay in Mexico was an enjoyable one both professionally and personally. I had the opportunity to work with the local security services to try to combat the growing drug threat and to enjoy life outside the Washington bubble. The assignment was not without some challenges. In April 1999, *Milenio,* a Mexican equivalent of *Time* magazine, came out with a four-page story all about me. The cover of the magazine had the CIA seal in the background, with the title "The New CIA Chief in Mexico is Jose Rodriguez."

For my entire CIA career, I had lived a life undercover. Those without a need to know (which included most people on the planet) were told that I worked for some other part of the U.S. government. Seeing your name and true occupation splashed across a major news magazine can be quite bracing for someone in my profession. Despite what Hollywood would have you believe, however, there *is* life and an intelligence career is possible after having your cover blown. My biggest concern was for the safety of my family. Mexico's narco traffickers would have liked nothing better than to exact revenge against the CIA's senior officer in their country. The Agency dispatched a surveillance team to keep watch on Patti and the boys. Essentially they would try to clandestinely follow them to make sure no bad guys were doing the same. The boys took great pleasure in trying to "spot the spooks" as Patti drove them to and from soccer practice. A short while later, after the surveillance was dropped, when I was out of the country on business, Patti and the boys returned from church one Sunday and discovered intruders in our home. It turned out they were burglars and not terrorists, but the experience was terrifying for them nonetheless.

But most of our family memories of Mexico City were positive ones. Both Nic and Alec discovered they shared my love of riding, and we enjoyed taking our horses, Azabache, Pancho, and Igotis, out on weekends and holidays. We stabled the horses near La Marquesa National Park on the outskirts of Mexico City, where we rode them with reckless abandon, jumping natural obstacles like fallen trees and ditches and galloping up and down the many beautiful valleys. By the time we left Mexico City, the boys were expert riders. It was very difficult to leave behind our beloved horses, but our memories of riding in Mexico City will be lasting ones.

After three years in Mexico City, I returned to headquarters to an uncertain future. When I got back to Langley I paid a visit to Jim Pavitt, the deputy director for Operations (known as the DDO). At the time he was the most senior officer in the clandestine service. I had known Jim for many years and enjoyed a solid personal and working relationship with him. Jim was complimentary about my performance in Mexico but was uncertain what they might do with me in the future. "Go home and take some of that leave you have built up," he said. "We'll find something for you to do," he added, somewhat unconvincingly. The date was early September 2001.

Patti and I were at home on September 11 unpacking some of the household goods that had just arrived after our move back to Virginia from Mexico. Sherry, a longtime friend and former neighbor of ours, called us distraught. "Put the television on! Put the television on!" she screamed. "The country is being attacked!" We immediately did as she instructed and sat transfixed as we watched the awful events in New York City and at the nearby Pentagon play out. As the awful scene unfolded before our eyes, I felt the outrage and the horror that all

Americans felt that morning. Watching the burning towers and the heart-wrenching scene of some of their occupants leaping to their deaths, I shared the desire held by all my countrymen that the dastardly attacks be avenged. But unlike most Americans, I had a chance to do something directly about it.

As Patti and I watched in stunned silence amid our moving boxes, my colleagues back at CIA headquarters were on the move. Many of them were sent home from work, because there were additional planes aloft that were unaccounted for and there had been previous al-Qa'ida threats to attack the Agency headquarters. A relatively small group of officers in the Agency's Counterterrorist Center (CTC) remained at their desks, desperately trying to find out who was behind the morning's attacks and what additional assaults might be on the horizon.

For the men and women of CTC, the events that morning were a doubly bitter blow. Like all Americans, they were shocked by what they saw, but like few others, they were not surprised, because they had been warning about and fighting against the al-Qa'ida target for years. Sometimes, seemingly alone in the U.S. government, they had been battling Usama bin Ladin and his cohorts for all those years. They were haunted by the knowledge that they had been unable to thwart the 9/11 attack, which had killed thousands of innocent men, women, and children.

A few days later I went back to Langley to discuss with my superiors my next assignment. Always a very securely guarded facility, the place was now bristling with new defenses. Armored Humvees with security officers carrying automatic weapons were everywhere, in a show of vigilance that was duplicated at prominent buildings all around the Washington area.

I made my way to the seventh floor, the part of the Agency occupied by CIA's seniormost leadership. All about me people were buzzing around with a redoubled sense of urgency. I could tell by the look in their eyes, and sometimes by the stubble on their chins, that many of my colleagues had had little sleep since the attacks on Tuesday morning. My message to Pavitt and his colleagues was a simple one: Put me in. I didn't care what I was given to do; I just wanted to contribute to the fight. My reaction was not unique. Hundreds of retired Agency officers, some recent, others long past their prime, dropped whatever they were doing and called headquarters offering to come back and pitch in. Some, unable to get through on the phone, just jumped into their cars and drove to Virginia and showed up at the gate ready to take on any mission.

As had been the case a few days before, Pavitt, the deputy director for Operations (the DDO), was still unclear exactly what he might ask me to do, but there was no question about where the need was greatest. "Go down to CTC," he said, "and help Cofer Black out." That kind of vague marching order is not typical in a bureaucracy, but this was no ordinary time.

Although I was no expert in counterterrorism, I had had lots of experience running relatively large operations for the Agency. At the time I was an SIS 4 (Senior Intelligence Service 4), equivalent to about a three-star general, and had commanded a Directorate of Operations division and large overseas stations. While the CIA is not a particularly rank-conscious organization, when you reach the upper levels of the Senior Intelligence Service, you are expected to be able to get things done, and quickly.

Cofer Black, my classmate from the Farm a quarter century before, certainly could use the help. Even as a junior officer, Cofer had carried himself with a style and class that set him apart. He speaks in cultured, measured (but often colorful) tones. Cofer always had a flair for the dramatic, and even when we were young trainees, I always thought he had his act together. He was married and settled while I was single and nomadic. I remember having dinner at his townhouse once and being amazed that he and his wife had china, real silverware, and drank wine from a bottle that did not have a screw-off top. I, on the other hand, was a bachelor living in a sublet studio apartment that contained just the bare essentials.

Now, twenty-five years later, Cofer held one of the most significant jobs in our profession. We had not had much contact since our training days. He had spent much of his career in Africa, just as I had spent mine in Latin America. It has been widely reported that Cofer was heavily responsible for the collection of intelligence that resulted in the capture of the terrorist Ilich Ramirez Sanchez, better known as "Carlos the Jackal," in Sudan in 1994.

Since mid-1999, Cofer had been chief of CTC. A "center" in Agency parlance (like the Crime and Narcotics Center I worked in during the midnineties) is an organization whose staffs include both operations officers and analysts as well as representatives from many other agencies across the intelligence community. In much of the rest of the Agency those two skill sets are largely separated. "Case officers" and their associates are the people who go out and collect intelligence and conduct operations. Analysts are the people who study that information plus the material gathered through other means, such as signals intelligence and open-source materials, and try to make sense of it.

In CTC the two cultures merge, often working side by side, leveraging the skills of one to help the other succeed. It was, as one of my colleagues described it, in a football analogy, like being fortunate enough to have the offense and the defense on the field at the same time.

Before 9/11, I don't think most people at the CIA would have described CTC as a small organization, but compared to what the public might imagine or compared to what it is today, it certainly was quite small. One of outsiders' big misconceptions is that the Agency is a large, omnipresent operation. Despite its worldwide responsibilities, the Agency has a fraction of the manpower of some of its counterparts. Before 9/11 there were more FBI special agents in New York City alone than the CIA had case officers around the globe.

At the time of 9/11, there were several hundred people assigned to CTC and a relatively small annual budget. Within months of the attacks on the World Trade Center the resources available would increase tenfold. No organization can handle such explosive growth without considerable pain, and that's where I came in.

While the smoke was still rising from the pile of rubble in New York and the gaping hole in the Pentagon, CIA Director George Tenet tapped Cofer to come up with a plan to go after al-Qa'ida and their Taliban protectors in Afghanistan and to bring to justice terrorists elsewhere around the world. Cofer and his team were able to quickly assemble such a plan because they had been working on it for years. Tenet and Black briefed President Bush and other senior administration officials at Camp David on Saturday, September 15.

While September 11 was undoubtedly the worst day in CIA history, September 15 turned out to be one of its best. On that day the CIA demonstrated that it had the knowhow and, most important, the nimbleness to come up with a workable operation that our highly capable but more lumbering colleagues at the Pentagon could scarcely match.

I arrived in CTC at a time of organized chaos. The sense of urgency was palpable. Most of the longest-serving officers were convinced that a second strike was imminent. No one knew where that might take place. Everything and everyone seemed vulnerable.

Walking into CTC's offices on the ground floor of the CIA's "new" headquarters building, which had been around for about a decade (as opposed to its neighbor, the "original" headquarters building, which opened in the early 1960s), one couldn't help but feel the sense of mission. Cofer was consumed with meetings at the White House and Pentagon and soon would launch on trips around the world to enlist allies in the war on terror. His able deputy, Ben Bonk, a brilliant analyst who, in addition to being one of the brightest people at the Agency, was hands down one of the nicest, was trying to get his arms around the flood of intelligence that was suddenly pouring in on the terrorist target. Ben spent most of his day at meetings "downtown," which is what we called the White House and State Department.

I had no clear job, no office, and no title, and neither Cofer nor Ben had time to help me find them. So I created them for myself. I had a copier machine moved out of a room not much bigger than a closet and created an office. I elected to call myself CTC's chief operating officer, since most of the other logical titles were taken. I jumped in and tried to make sense of the influx of added people, dollars, and, most important, missions that were coming CTC's way. Cofer and Ben welcomed the help and gave me all the latitude I could want. I never experienced either before or since such a sense of teamwork.

Director Tenet and his deputy, John McLaughlin, had directed that CTC get whatever it needed in the way of resources. We had only to ask. Knowing what to ask for, and where to get it, proved to be a challenge. Normally when there is a surge situation, the parts of the organization that lose some of their people, turf, and mission put up a fight. Not this time. When we asked for something from other offices and directorates within the Agency and for people to be detailed from other parts of the government to us, the answer was always "you bet."

Bruce Pease, another of the Agency's top analysts, was brought in to set up a new analytical structure within CTC called the Office of Terrorism Analysis. It was based on an existing unit of twenty to thirty people but needed to expand rapidly, growing to almost three hundred people. Bruce decided that we did not have time to bring in lots of people as individuals and train them to work against the terrorist target while simultaneously training them to work together as a unit. So a plan was developed to go to the Directorate of Intelligence, the home of the analysts, and draft entire teams. We grabbed entire units that one day might have been in charge of doing political analysis for Eastern Europe or perhaps Southeast Asia and moved them lock, stock, and barrel to CTC. Senior officers to the newest analytical recruit were moved en masse.

On the operational side we pulled the best people we could find from units across the Agency. We also grabbed the entire output of our clandestine training facility, the Farm, and threw them into the fight. Suddenly cadres of men and women detailed to us from the Pentagon, NSA, DIA, and elsewhere started showing up on our doorstep.

I was blown away by the ability and dedication of the people we were bringing together. But if there was one group or category of individual that was most impressive, hands down, it was our women officers. I never met such a determined, focused, and capable group of people. You couldn't help but notice that so many of the key decision-making positions in CTC were filled by women. I recruited several of our key performers from elsewhere in the Agency. One woman, whom I'll call "Sara," had worked with me a few years before in the Agency's Crime and Narcotics Center (CNC). As Sara put it, she and I had "done drugs" together in the basement where the CNC was located. She was a whiz at organization and, more than any other single individual, was responsible for rewiring

CTC to handle its explosive growth in mission and resources. When she got to CTC we were drowning in paper. We had only one person assigned to answer the mail and one to handle budgets, and we had no earthly idea how many people actually worked in our organization, which had suddenly been flooded with fresh talent. Sara built a structure that allowed us to work at maximum efficiency.

Another superstar whom I recruited was "Jane," who had served extensive time overseas and was working in an Agency organization that provided surveillance support. I stole her away and had her head one of our earliest "black sites," where terrorists were interrogated. Later she became my right arm as chief of staff when I led the clandestine service. Both Sara and Jane went on to very high-ranking positions within the Agency, positions that they still serve in today. I owe a lot of my success to their hard work and dedication.

Just as we were grabbing people, we commandeered physical space. Wide spots in hallways became administrative centers, conference rooms became command centers, and small rooms that once housed two or three officers suddenly became home to dozens.

Cofer delegated to me much of the organization and management of the dramatic growth. He simply didn't have time to deal with it. He also had little patience with the myriad meetings on the seventh floor and quickly deputized me to attend a 7:30 a.m. daily session in Jim Pavitt's office.

At 5:00 p.m. each day there was a remarkable meeting in the director's conference room at which Cofer, Ben, and I, along with a dozen or more of our key people, would meet with Tenet, McLaughlin, and Pavitt to manage our counterterrorism efforts. In all my years in government, I never saw a meeting like that one. There were countless important decisions made and orders given at that session with little time for debate and no time for dithering. The DCI conference room was packed with people who could make stuff happen, and regularly people were sent, often literally running out of the room, to implement a decision that came down from the top.

Only a small percentage of CTC officers were in that room, but down in our spaces on the ground floor, everyone was expected to contribute and innovate. Senior leaders like Bruce Pease would cram his troops into the biggest office they could find and stand on a chair to be seen and heard by those in attendance. "I don't have time to tell each of you what to do," he said on many occasions. "We expect everyone to innovate and to exercise greater leadership and responsibility than you have ever before." They did.

We were very much flying by the seat of our pants. At one five o'clock meeting, Pease gave the DCI a quick status report on the influx of new analysts into CTC. "It's working," he said, "but we are going to make some mistakes." Tenet looked at Bruce and then the rest of CTC's leadership and said: "We can't afford mistakes. Mistakes will kill us." He probably had in mind the second-guessing that had become rampant in the months after 9/11, much of it by people who had ignored CTC's warnings about al-Qa'ida before September 11, and who were now suddenly asking why the Agency had not done more to prevent the attacks. More than being directed at the CIA as an institution, Tenet's caution was a reminder that lapses by our analysts could easily result in the deaths of thousands more Americans. We couldn't promise Tenet we would not make analytical and operational mistakes in the future, but the message was received. We had to do everything in our power to prevent them.

Terrorism has always been one of the toughest targets on which to collect intelligence. Unlike the old Soviet Union, where the things to keep track of (tanks, ships, missiles, and so on) were big, the things counterterrorist analysts are concerned with are small, often single individuals. And the secrets you want to steal frequently don't reside in computer systems that can be hacked, or safes that can be broken into, but in the inner recesses of a handful of individuals' minds.

Yet by dint of hard work, the cooperation of allies and even former enemies around the world, and the application of some new tools, we were suddenly awash in data. The problem was making sense of it.

The cliché about intelligence work is that doing intelligence is like working on a thousand-piece jigsaw puzzle but not having the box top to tell you what the finished picture should look like. If only it were that easy. In fact, it is more like working on a million-piece puzzle, with no box top, and having millions more random pieces that look like they might fit, but actually are from different puzzles altogether.

It fell to us to make sense of the countless fragments of information and to take action on the chunks of the puzzle that represented a real and growing threat to the United States and our allies.

I remember going into a room that a few weeks before had been the CTC conference room. Now it was a command and data triage center. Every seat along the lengthy conference table had a computer in front of it. Scores of cables snaked their way down the center of the table and under the floor. Each computer had a cardboard name plate with a hand-scrawled ID to tell others what function the person in that seat filled. Many in the room had not yet met each other a few days before. Also strewn about the room were pairs of telephones color coded to let the users know which ones were for unclassified conversations and which were for talking to colleagues around the world on sensitive classified matters. The unclassified phones (known as "black lines") did not get much of a workout other than to let spouses know that their loved one was going to miss dinner yet again. Walking into the room you were hit by a cacophony of noise that one officer described as being like having to work at Chuck E. Cheese.

While there was often a sense of creative chaos, there was no doubt about what we were trying to accomplish. Less than a week after 9/11, the president provided us with written authorization that allowed us to capture, render, and interrogate terrorists. As with all such authorizations, these documents are the bedrock of what we could and could not legally do as an organization. They were briefed to the congressional leadership, who, to a man and woman, expressed no objection, even to the very specific authorization of what we could do against al-Qa'ida operatives. Armed with new authorities and with the full backing of a united government and the American people, we went to war.

Chapter 3

ABU ZUBAYDAH

The CIA had been deeply concerned about bin Ladin's organization since at least 1996, when we set up a small unit specifically designed to target a group that was known as "the base," or al-Qa'ida, but we did not know nearly enough about the shadowy organization. The unit pursued bin Ladin's outfit vigorously around the globe. And although they learned much about al-Qa'ida, by 9/11 it was still an organization that remained quite mysterious to us. We did not have the human source penetration of the organization required and had an inadequate understanding of it below Usama bin Ladin. Moreover, we did not have a good grasp on what other individuals among its leadership were doing, nor did we have a deep understanding of al-Qa'ida's objectives and capabilities for transcontinental attack.

There was one notable exception to our shallow base of knowledge. There was a Palestinian who grew up in Saudi Arabia by the name of Zayn al-Abidin Muhammad Husayn, better known as Abu Zubaydah. To us, he quickly and simply became "AZ." We had been chasing him for years. He spoke openly on phone lines and used email to communicate with fellow operatives, so he was one of the al-Qa'ida senior figures on whom we had collected considerable intelligence. We knew him to be a premier recruiter and facilitator for bin Ladin's organization and knew he had been involved in a December 1999 Millennium Plot that, had it not been thwarted by the U.S. and Arab partners, would have killed hundreds of innocent people in the U.S., Jordan, and elsewhere.

After Ahmad Ressam was captured by an alert U.S. customs

agent as he was trying to sneak across the Canadian border into the U.S. in late 1999, he told the FBI that AZ was among those planning multiple attacks against U.S. cities.

And when George Tenet, Cofer Black, and several top CTC officers visited Condi Rice at the White House in July 2001 with "their hair on fire" to warn about pending al-Qa'ida attacks against U.S. interests, one of the prime names they cited was Abu Zubaydah.

So it was not surprising that following the attacks of 9/11, AZ would have been on the top of our list of most wanted enemies. We knew that following the failed Millennium attacks he had sought a haven in Afghanistan. After the CIA-led efforts to rout al-Qa'ida and the Taliban in the fall of 2001, we assumed that AZ, like much of the rest of his organization's leadership, had fled across the mountainous border to Pakistan. But he had gone "radio silent."

Then in early 2002 he came back "on the air" again. We could tell he was in Pakistan but had little indication where among that country's 170 million people he was hiding.

As troublesome as the U.S.-Pakistani relationship was in the 1990s, and as difficult as it has become in recent years, it is important to remember that in the days immediately after 9/11, Pakistan's government made the strategic decision to come to the aid of the United States. Then-President Musharraf took some critical concrete steps, such as replacing the head of ISI, and directing that the military and paramilitary cooperate with the U.S.

No doubt this assistance was undertaken with self-protection in mind. But for whatever reason, Musharraf and his top aides correctly read the handwriting on the wall and cast their lot with the Americans. That decision became especially important as we tried to track down elements of al-Qa'ida's senior leadership, many of whom we believed were hiding in his country's highly populated urban areas.

It is hard to overstate the urgency we felt in getting our hands on some of bin Ladin's top deputies. Intercepted communications both before and after 9/11 gave the clear impression that additional, even more spectacular attacks were planned. The anthrax attacks in the United States only heightened fears that mass killings using unconventional means were indeed possible and perhaps already under way. Confirmed reports that al-Qa'ida was seeking nuclear material and had access to rogue Pakistani nuclear scientists raised our legitimate concerns exponentially.

In early 2002, Director Tenet asked CTC to brief him on our efforts to find and capture Abu Zubaydah. Cofer Black and several of our top people told Tenet that we believed AZ was moving around the cities of Faisalabad, Islamabad, Peshawar, and Karachi. It is not hard to tell when George has been underwhelmed in a briefing, and this was one of those occasions. He let Cofer know in no uncertain terms that we had to do better.

It wasn't long after Cofer made the trip from Tenet's seventh-floor office to our warren of cubicles on the ground floor that changes started to happen. Our lone conference room was reconfigured again. Now it became home to the Abu Zubaydah Task Force. Twenty-five computer terminals were crammed into the twenty-five-foot-by-fifteen-foot conference room, and we assembled a team of people whose sole mission in life was to find and capture AZ.

To lead the effort we selected Jennifer Matthews, a no-nonsense officer in her midthirties. A bundle of energy, Jennifer was passionate about her job. She would literally tremble with excitement when things were going well at work. She was one of CTC's most effective, dedicated, and successful officers. Originally an imagery analyst, she shifted to the clandestine side of the Agency and became an operations officer following graduation with top honors from the FTCC Field Tradecraft Course in 2000. Jennifer's skill set now bridged the two main cultures within CTC, the analysts and the operators.

At the time of this assignment Jennifer was well along in her pregnancy with her third child. Somehow, however, she managed to balance a family life with total dedication to her operational mission. Jennifer worked closely with senior Agency officers in Pakistan, feeding them information on details we were able to elicit at headquarters and demanding from them additional information that could be collected only in the field to help piece together the puzzle.

The job of finding AZ was largely a case of sifting through mountains of technical information to pinpoint his location. This required calling on the skills of several other U.S. intelligence agencies. AZ was not making it easy on us. He seemed to have learned from his earlier days, when his operational tradecraft was considerably sloppier. Now he was constantly changing locations, using different cell phones, communicating through surrogates, and connecting on the web by one-time visits to obscure internet cafés.

To carry out her mission, Jennifer led a large team that worked around the clock for three weeks. Operational leads were coming in from Pakistan on a twenty-four-hour basis and needed to be analyzed and exploited by the AZ Task Force without a moment's delay.

While Jennifer was given several experienced senior managers to help run the task force, it was a labor-intensive operation, and much of the "critical mass" came from young officers who had been with the CIA for less than a year. These trainees were recent hires who were getting a crash course in Agency life even before they went off for operational training.

Jennifer masterfully led her young workforce, motivating them to dedicate the countless hours necessary to sift through the reams of operational data to help identify possible patterns of AZ's travels and communications.

The CIA had a parallel organization in the field. We had learned the value of sending analysts "downrange" in situations like this to push information and leads in both directions. In the region we had ten people crammed into a room that should have held two, working on the Abu Zubaydah hunt.

The link analysis quickly began to offer hope. As AZ's trail got hotter, I remember Jennifer briefing Director Tenet several times at our critical five-o'clock meeting on what she was finding. Being an inclusive leader, she often would let one of her trainees address the group. Imagine being just six months out of college and finding yourself face-to-face with the director of the CIA, briefing him on a matter of enormous importance to U.S. national security. The young officers would go back down seven floors to CTC's cramped conference room inspired to work even harder in their relentless search.

While we were making good progress in narrowing the hunt for AZ, the effort still had very much a "needle-in-the-haystack" feel to it. There was a technical device that I am not at liberty to describe further that would help. Tenet ordered that every device be ripped away from wherever it was and devoted to the AZ hunt.

To augment maps received from the CIA's extensive map library, Agency officers in Islamabad went to a local bookstore and bought every map they could find of cities, including Faisalabad. Pinning the maps to the wall, they started plotting possible target locations and exchanged daily situation reports with Jennifer's operation at HQ.

By mid-March, the intense collection effort had yielded about sixteen locations where AZ might conceivably be. On March 17 there was a terrorist attack on a church in Islamabad that killed a U.S. State Department employee and wounded her two children and husband. As a result, the FBI sent a bunch of special agents to Pakistan, and they were quickly folded into our anti-AZ effort.

Working with our Pakistani partners, we decided to raid all sixteen sites simultaneously. With the recent influx of FBI special agents, we now had enough U.S. assets to have people at each target site along with the Pakistanis. The decision to go after all the sites at once was unusual but if we had worked through them one by one, he would likely have found out that we were closing in on him and fled the area entirely. There were reports that Abu Zubaydah planned to relocate to Iran, so time was of the essence. We started gathering more data about each location. The address of one location turned out essentially to be a vacant lot. It would have been understandable to write that one off as a technical glitch and to focus solely on the other sites. But one of our Pakistani liaisons explained to our officers in the field that it was common practice in the area for people to steal telephone lines. What they would do was tap into a nearby phone line and run their own "pirate" line to a home or business where they could enjoy anonymous (and free) phone service. Our Pakistani colleague visited the vacant lot, climbed a telephone pole, and followed an unofficial phone line to a nearby building. That site remained on the target list.

As the hunt heated up, Director Tenet briefed the White House staff on the progress. He took Jennifer Matthews to the White House Situation Room to brief National Security Advisor Condoleezza Rice. Jennifer walked through the simultaneous takedown operation, explaining the complex way she and her colleagues had collected, synthesized, and exploited all available intelligence to come up with the list. She highlighted for Rice how helpful the Pakistanis had been. As White House officials are wont to do, Rice asked Jennifer what the odds were on AZ's being captured as part of this operation. Given his propensity for moving around and constantly changing locations, Jennifer placed the chance of success at no more than 40 percent.

The raids were set for about 1:00 a.m. Pakistani time on March 28. As it turned out, given the time difference, they were taking place while we were in Director Tenet's five-o'clock meeting. We didn't expect to hear even preliminary results until a little later, but the thoughts of many of us were half a world away. A few minutes before the meeting concluded, Jennifer burst into the DCI's conference room with a gaggle of breathless trainees behind her. She read a brief email from a CIA team leader in Faisalabad. The raid on the house identified by our Pakistani liaison following a pirate phone line resulted in a shootout. One individual was seriously wounded by a Pakistani-U.S. pursuit team while attempting to jump from one building's roof to another while firing an AK-47. Initial reports said he had been shot three times. Although his identity was unconfirmed, Agency officers on the scene said he looked an awful lot like the man they had been pursuing, Abu Zubaydah.

We later learned that one of AZ's associates, a Libyan, was killed in the raid, and that at least one escaped. That individual was later believed to have been involved in the killing of a U.S. diplomat, Lawrence Foley, in Jordan.

As I recall, there was no applause in the conference room, no high fives for sure. But there was a sense of satisfaction that, if the reports were true, we had just achieved the biggest victory in the long battle since 9/11 by capturing the highest-level al-Qa'ida terrorist we ever had.

Immediately, Jennifer and her team went back to their conference room/command center and continued the tedious but rewarding work of following the trail and exploiting the information that had just come into our hands.

Jennifer Matthews was emblematic of the terrific officers

who worked in CTC. As significant as her contributions were, I doubt I would be telling you her name today (such are the concerns of secrecy) except for the fact that on December 30, 2009, she was continuing the fight against al-Qa'ida by serving as chief of base at a CIA facility in Khost, Afghanistan. There, she and six other Agency officers and a Jordanian intelligence service liaison were killed by an al-Qa'ida suicide bomber. To the very end of her life, she was leading in the fight against our murderous foes.

Abu Zubaydah's capture and its aftermath soon became the subject of legend. As with most legends, much of what is said is false. Some of the myths came from our own colleagues. One former CIA analyst even wrote a book suggesting that he led the whole operation and was present when AZ was taken down. In fact, that officer was said by some to have been hours away, observing one of the nonfruitful raids, but has since made a career out of implying that the AZ victory was of his making.

The real success of the Abu Zubaydah takedown allowed us to use the same methodology over and over again. When AZ was captured, we also were able to seize his computer, phones, writings, and lots of other material that helped inform our future efforts.

Given his importance, a decision was made to exploit the captured material (a process known as document exploitation) at CIA headquarters. While tons of critically important material was discovered, the process also led to one uncomfortable moment. Included among the material that was quickly packed up and shipped back to headquarters was a piece of live ordnance. When it was discovered, security was called. One of our best analysts recalls sitting in his office when someone came along stringing a piece of yellow tape across his desk. "What's this?" he asked. "Oh, we found a piece of unexploded ordnance next door," he was told. The analyst decided this might be an excellent time to go to the cafeteria for a cup of coffee.

Before capturing Abu Zubaydah, when it came to holding and interrogating terrorists, the CIA often relied on a procedure known as "rendition." Like so many things the Agency has been involved with, renditions have been the subject of myth and misunderstanding.

Conventional wisdom these days is that renditions were an invention of the Bush administration in order to allow suspected terrorists to be snatched off the street and taken to third countries, where they would be tortured. That's just not so. The technique has been in use for many years, going back at least to the Reagan administration. It reached its zenith during the Clinton administration, when some seventy people around the world were subjected to rendition.

During the nineties many terrorists were picked up in one part of the world, almost always with the active or tacit cooperation of the country in which they were living, and spirited to another location at which they might be wanted for crimes. Often the place they ended up was their home country. Sometimes it was a country against which they plotted or one that had special insights into the group to which the terrorist belonged. Occasionally, they were brought to the United States if there was an active warrant for their arrest, as was the case, for example, with Aimal Kasi, a Pakistani man who shot and killed two CIA officers and wounded three others outside the Agency headquarters in January 1993. Kasi was picked up in Pakistan in 1997, brought back to the United States, stood trial, and was executed in November 2002.

More often than not, however, the prospect of a conviction in the U.S. was not so clear-cut, and it was deemed more productive to disrupt the terrorist's plans by transferring him to a third country. Agency critics and the media invented a new term, "extraordinary rendition," to refer to this effort. To us a rendition was a rendition, and we never used that phrase. The rendition process was used quite regularly during the Clinton administration, and those who regularly briefed Congress on the program tell me they never heard any opposition to it.

In the early days after 9/11, we continued to use the program. An al-Qa'ida operative who went by the name of Ibn al Shaykh al-Libi was captured in Pakistan in late 2001. He was picked up along with other Arabs who were fleeing Afghanistan and the massive U.S. bombing at Tora Bora aimed at getting bin Ladin. Al-Libi was believed to have been the director of an al-Qa'ida training camp in Afghanistan. Someone in that position would be well equipped to tell interrogators about people who had passed through the camp, plots that had been hatched there, and support al-Qa'ida had received. But at this initial stage of the war we were so swamped with the business of routing the Taliban from Afghanistan that it was thought best that we pass al-Libi along to the Egyptians, who might be able to get the most out of his interrogation. As always with renditions to a third country, the CIA insisted that the receiving country promise not to abuse the detainee, but to a large extent we had to rely on the host country's assurances. In the case of al-Libi, we were not that comfortable. The results that the Egyptians passed to us from his interrogation were problematic. Although they did pass along a lot of threat information about various al-Qa'ida plots, there was a notable lack of follow-up or detail in their questioning. The Egyptians had their own priorities.

Eventually al-Libi did provide some explosive information, including allegations that al-Qa'ida had worked with Russian organized-crime syndicates to try to bring "canisters" of nuclear material into the United States. He also told the Egyptians that al-Qa'ida operatives had been in touch with Iraq to obtain training on the use of poisons. This information eventually made its way into Secretary of State Powell's early 2003 presentation to the U.N. justifying action against Iraq.

But al-Libi later recanted much of the information he supplied, including the stories about nuclear material and cooperation with the Iraqis. Since we were not present when the information was offered, we didn't know if he was lying in the first instance or the second. That kind of uncertainty made those of us in CTC very uncomfortable about contracting out the interrogation of some of our most important detainees. We couldn't control interviews done by others, had limited ability to ask time-urgent follow-on questions, and quite significantly, could not guarantee that the prisoner's rights were being respected. And therefore we pushed for the establishment of our own detention and interrogation facilities, the "black sites"—facilities in a third country where detainees could be held and questioned in secrecy.

It is more than a little ironic that the secret detention facilities that the CIA established, at which we have been widely accused of abusing prisoners, were established in part for the express purpose of making sure that these critical detainees were not mistreated.

The rendition program did not end with the establishment of the black sites. It continued to be valuable in a select group of cases in which our capacity to interrogate certain prisoners had been maxed out or a third country had some special understanding of or connection with the detainee that made it the best choice to question someone. We continued to do all we could to insist that prisoners were not abused. Not every rendition was well-handled or well-advised, however. There are a few cases that have become notorious, some with good reason. But the vast majority of rendition cases were handled appropriately and produced valuable intelligence. Most of them you have never heard of. None, however, produced the kind of critical intelligence that we got when we established our own capability.

Our first concern after capturing Abu Zubaydah was keeping him alive. It wasn't easy. The single bullet that had penetrated his thigh when he was captured had hit bone and ricocheted around his body, causing multiple injuries so severe that initially people thought he had been hit by as many as three bullets. The CIA made arrangements for a world-class surgeon from Johns Hopkins Medical Center to be dispatched by private jet to Pakistan to make sure our prize prisoner survived. It was a near-run thing.

AZ lapsed in and out of consciousness several times and only the combination of the surgeon's skill and our good luck brought him through. There were several occasions when he nearly died.

CIA officers and FBI agents remained at his side, both for his protection and to be alert in case AZ blurted out something useful in his delirium. As it became clear that AZ's survival was probable, it became equally clear that we had to get him out of Pakistan. Too many people of questionable loyalty knew who he was and where he was being held.

We immediately went to work to identify and establish a black site. We believed it critical to be able to conduct the interrogations in isolation, with neither the detainee nor the rest of the world knowing where he was. Working with a friendly country, we were able to quickly establish a facility that had the attributes we wanted. It was accessible but remote, defendable, and the comings and goings of Agency officers and their "guests" would not easily attract attention. We wanted to be able to hide in plain sight. To our potential hosts we promised three things: our gratitude, a sizable amount of money, and our assurances that we would do everything in our power to keep their support secret. We were eventually able to deliver only two out of the three.

Shortly after we got an agreement from an allied country to

host the black site, I flew out myself to check on its construction. Abu Zubaydah was already present in a hospital-like room where he was being carefully treated for his wounds. Nearby, a holding facility was under construction, which would allow us to interrogate him in complete isolation. We believed it important that Abu Zubaydah and the detainees who followed him not know where they were and took great efforts to ensure that was the case. We quickly were able to ready a holding facility for our guest that awaited only his recovery to good health for us to begin to use. The living conditions for our personnel who would operate the facility were spartan as well, but given the importance of the task at hand, I was confident that none of them would complain.

The CIA had had for some time working on contract for it a civilian psychologist who had had extensive experience working with the U.S. military's SERE (Survival, Evasion, Resistance, and Escape) program.

Within two days of AZ's capture, we tracked down the contractor and asked if he would accompany a team of CTC officers to the black site where we hoped Abu Zubaydah would be interrogated. The contractor's role was not to lead the interrogation but to advise our officers and on-scene FBI agents about any counterinterrogation techniques AZ might be employing to avoid providing critical data.

In recent years, after the detention and interrogation of al-Qa'ida operatives has gotten considerable negative publicity, one former FBI special agent in particular has been aggressively telling stories about how he and his colleagues got all the good information out of AZ and how they could have gotten more but were thwarted by their brutish counterparts from the CIA. The truth is quite different.

One of the myths about the CIA's views on terrorist interrogation is that our position is that the bad guys say absolutely nothing when first captured and that after we literally twist their arms they suddenly tell everything they know. That is not how it worked.

CIA officers and two FBI agents were with AZ constantly while he drifted in and out of consciousness. Not knowing if he would live or die, they tried to ask him questions during periods of lucidity.

After overcoming the shock of being captured, most detainees talked a little. Some talked a lot. Most tried to feed their captors information that they thought would give the impression they were cooperating but would result in no significant intelligence gain. Often they underestimated us. Such was the case with AZ in the early stages of his detention.

At one point he said to the senior CIA officer present and another FBI agent that he had "just remembered" something he wanted to tell them about "dirty bombs" but that he was exhausted and needed eight hours of sleep. They consulted with our contractor, who suggested that they let AZ sleep for four hours, then wake him and tell him he had been asleep for eight. If he indeed had information about dirty bombs, they didn't want to waste any time finding out about it.

When AZ awoke he provided a very vague description of two colleagues who he said were planning on conducting a terrorist operation in the United States. One he called "Abu al-Amerikani." The information he was sharing was very sketchy, and Abu Zubaydah undoubtedly believed that it was so imprecise that we would never be able to locate the person he was talking about. Fortunately, due to some exceptional intelligence work by CIA officers in Pakistan, which allowed us to identify that person (a U.S. citizen by the name of Jose Padilla), we were able to locate him overseas and have him tracked until he reached Chicago's O'Hare Airport, where he was arrested. While successfully conducting a dirty bomb attack turned out to be beyond Padilla's capabilities, he definitely had the desire and intent to conduct some sort of mass-casualty attack on the United States and was thwarted only by good luck and good intelligence work.

While we were delighted to have this early success, we were confident that Abu Zubaydah knew much, much more, and we could not count on similar slips by him to give us what we needed to know in any timely manner.

In the early days of AZ's detention, there were essentially three different types of interrogation being conducted simultaneously. The two FBI agents employed their standard methods, generally designed to get people to confess to crimes so that they can be prosecuted. They called this "informed interrogation" and used all the standard techniques, such as "good cop–bad cop," attempts at rapport building, and pretending that they knew more than they did. Also present was a senior officer from the CIA's office of security who had conducted countless investigations himself and tended to prefer a law enforcement nine-step technique known as the Reid Method. Finally, there was a senior CIA operations officer who had vast experience in foreign intelligence and whose standard procedures were designed to elicit intelligence, not convictions. All three techniques have their virtues and successes. All of the participants worked as a team and were advised by our contractor.

For the most part the CIA officers and FBI agents present got along well and worked together collegially. Where there were differences, they were largely ones of divergent perspectives developed over years of experience in one culture or another. The FBI's mind-set is generally to gather information in such a way that it can be used to prove a crime in a trial. CIA officers' focus is on gathering intelligence to prevent future acts of terrorism. To some extent, for a handful of participants, the debate over primacy of interrogation techniques became a turf battle. And when the FBI didn't win that debate, some of its adherents never got over the fact.

Despite the current claims by former FBI agents that they had bonded with AZ and were able to charm information out of him, the facts are quite different. One of the FBI agents mistakenly revealed to AZ that we had his lengthy personal diary and were mining it for information. That cost us the benefit of surprise, which had allowed us to stun our detainee with things we knew about his past. That diary also proved to be the source of more controversy. Some in the FBI later told gullible journalists that it demonstrated that Abu Zubaydah was crazy. In fact, our analysis showed that he used a number of clever literary devices in expressing himself, but if anything, he was crazy like a fox.

Critics have said that AZ was not nearly as significant a player as we portrayed him as being. The truth, however, is that he was perfectly placed to answer the questions we had. As an al-Qa'ida facilitator, he knew all the major players in the organization. He knew where they came from, where they went, who they worked with, what they looked like, and how they were motivated. If you could have picked one person associated with al-Qa'ida at the time to interrogate, other than bin Ladin and his deputy, Ayman al-Zawahiri, themselves, it would have been Abu Zubaydah. Not only was he on our radar for plots against the United States, but he was also believed to have been behind a plot that was narrowly thwarted in Amman, Jordan, in December 1999, which involved huge amounts of explosives that could have killed thousands. As a Palestinian, AZ wanted to strike out against Jordan for "selling out" to Israel. Critics mistakenly assume that you have to nab the top person in a terrorist organization to stop a plot. The truth is that one of the best ways to disrupt terrorists is to know something about the group's organizational plumbing so that you can identify the critical nodes that, if attacked, will derail planning and plot preparations. This was the kind of knowledge that AZ had to a greater degree than almost anyone else at this point in al-Qa'ida's evolution.

AZ told CIA interrogators that he respected all of our team, especially the female chief of base (whom he called "the Emira," Arabic for "princess" or "leader") of the black site. He respected them all, he said, except for a Muslim FBI agent, who had offended him early on. The agent, it turned out, had tried to debate Islamic theory with AZ, who thought the agent had insufficient grounding in the facts.

At one point the Bureau guys decided to try to "recruit" AZ. In a meeting with the terrorist, the Arab-American agent told AZ, "Don't pay attention to those CIA people . . . you work with me," and he gave him a candy bar. AZ was offended that the agent would think that he could be bought for a Snickers bar. The FBI man tried to use his Arab heritage as an opening to get AZ to talk, but it turned out to be counterproductive. "You are the worst kind of Arab," AZ told him, "you are a traitor!" "Look," the FBI agent told him, "America knows who its friends and who its enemies are. Work with us and we can make you a wealthy man." AZ responded, "What makes you think I would turn my back on Allah for money?"

Another red herring that is sometimes thrown out is that technically, AZ was not a full-fledged member of al-Qa'ida. He had never sworn *bayat,* or allegiance, to bin Ladin. This is a meaningless distinction. Many senior operatives, including Khalid Sheikh Mohammed, the mastermind of 9/11, for various reasons did not become card-carrying members of UBL's organization, but there were no more important participants in its deadly deeds.

One FBI agent told CIA officers before going into an interrogation session that he planned to "go Sipowicz on Abu

Zubaydah." Our officer didn't catch the cultural reference, but the agent was referring to Andy Sipowicz, a character in the 1980s TV show *NYPD Blue*. Sipowicz, as played by Dennis Franz, was a hot-tempered, alcoholic bully who broke the rules but got results. True to his word, the FBI man entered AZ's holding cell and started screaming at him, calling him a "motherf***er" and a "son of a bitch." Abu Zubaydah, who speaks decent English, apparently mentally translated the slurs literally and later said that the G-man was calling his mother "a dog." That is not a recommended technique for bonding with Arab men, who view dogs as particularly unclean and loathsome animals.

Another FBI special agent tried the opposite approach, telling AZ that if he cooperated we would make sure his mother was well taken care of. "Stay away from my mother," he said, "if she thought I was cooperating with you she would be ashamed of me." The conversation illustrated one of the many differences between the typical criminal and a terrorist. Drug runners, for example, are not involved with narcotics for philosophical reasons—they are in it for the money. Terrorists are ideological revolutionaries. Their commitment to their cause is far more deeply rooted, and it takes a far different approach to get them to intentionally share valuable information.

The ham-handed approach of the FBI officers led to AZ's shutting down communication completely. The FBI agents appeared to realize the damage done and went back into his cell to try to restore relations. One of them even got down on the floor, held his hand, and apologized. AZ was not buying it. CIA officers watching on closed-circuit video saw Abu Zubaydah grab his own crotch, in a gesture more typical of American gangs than Islamic terrorists, and say, "You guys might as well go home because I am done with you."

• • •

CIA expert analysts, including Jennifer Matthews, were convinced that AZ had a ton of useful information in his head that could save American and allied lives. So the CIA team started to employ some techniques designed to get AZ to reconsider his decision to clam up. These techniques, such as limited sleep deprivation, isolation, bombarding his cell with noise, and the like, did not require special approval but went beyond something that a typical detainee in a U.S. prison might experience.

These actions seemed to upset at least one of our FBI colleagues, who made a play to take control of the interrogation. He got very confrontational and seemed to blame our contractor for everything. At the time the contractor was still just an advisor. He was not in charge of the interrogation and hadn't even received all the security clearances to allow him to read the most highly classified cable traffic flowing to and from the black site.

At one point, after being rebuffed at an interrogation attempt with AZ, the FBI agent threatened violence, not against Abu Zubaydah but against the contractor. He eventually calmed down and apologized, blaming his outburst on being "hot-blooded." He didn't stay calm for long, however, and eventually departed the black site, saying he did not want to be part of such procedures.

The FBI had talked about bringing in a "clean team"— a group of agents who were not privy to whatever AZ had previously said while he was in detention, nor would they know anything about how he had been treated. They hoped that he would repeat some of the things he had previously told us so that it would be useful in an eventual court case. But those of us in the CIA weren't focused on punishing him for the last atrocity; we wanted to stop the next one.

It was clear to us that we had to do something to get the

information flowing from AZ again. In June I asked several senior members of our AZ interrogation team, including the contractor, to come back to CIA HQ and meet with me. I listened to their descriptions of the successes and failures during the first two months of Abu Zubaydah's confinement and was convinced that we could not sit around forever and wait for AZ to have a change of heart, forget the insults of the FBI, and decide he wanted to trade his principles for a candy bar. We were under the constant threat of new and even more deadly attacks and time was of the essence.

Still, there were no guarantees. I asked the contractor how long it would take, if we employed more aggressive, but legal, techniques, before he would know whether a detainee was willing to cooperate or was so dedicated that he would take any secrets he had with him to the grave. "Thirty days" was his estimate. I thought about it overnight and the next morning asked the contractor if he would be willing to take charge of creating and implementing such a program. He said he would be willing to undertake the assignment but could not do it by himself. It was clear to me at that point that including the FBI in the interrogation, given their "prosecution at all cost" mentality, was not the way to go. I agreed that the contractor should bring in someone from the outside to help him work with Agency officers in crafting a program that we hoped would save lives.

The result was, beyond a doubt, the most effective and carefully managed program I was involved with in my thirty-one years at the CIA. But I also say that without doubt it remains the most maligned, misunderstood, and mischaracterized mission in the Agency's mystery-clouded history.

Here is how it began. The normal kinds of interrogation used by law enforcement, in our view, were not appropriate. Standard methods of police interrogation work well when trying to build a case for prosecution and when dealing with criminals who are motivated by a desire to minimize potential prison sentences or to expiate a sense of guilt. The people we were hoping to interrogate had no such expectations or feelings. Additionally, the more traditional "Reid technique" of interrogation broadly used by law enforcement agencies in the United States can work well when you have all the time in the world to employ it. We didn't have that luxury. We feared and anticipated a second wave of devastating attacks on the United States. You couldn't see a time bomb, but we could not miss the sound of one ticking.

We had two priorities. Any interrogation program we developed had to be effective and legal. Assuring ourselves of the latter proved time-consuming. But as critically important as we felt it to be to get information that might help us thwart impending attacks, I insisted that we take no action unless and until we were assured, in writing, by the seniormost legal authorities, that we were not crossing legal red lines. Some of my most senior leaders in CTC argued that we couldn't afford to wait for approval from policymakers. They felt the pressure of a possible second wave of attacks that might happen at any moment and knew that Abu Zubaydah had in his head information that could help us thwart them. But I said, no, we will not go ahead until we know we have the backing of our political leaders and a binding legal opinion from the Department of Justice.

In meeting after meeting at the White House, George Tenet insisted that there be buy-in both from the political leadership and from the top authorities at DOJ. He ensured that we kept the senior leadership of our congressional oversight committees informed as well. The pressure that we all felt from the administration and Congress was palpable. Perhaps even more so than we were, they were worried about an imminent next strike and wanted us to get critical information from the detainees to prevent it. But George insisted at one of our meetings: "We have to get this right or we will rue the day."

We got DOJ and White House authorization to begin the urgent interrogation of Abu Zubaydah in August of that year. Congress was in recess. Immediately upon their return I led a team from CTC that went to the Hill to brief the seniormost members of our oversight committees on this highly classified program. A briefing was given on September 4, 2002, to the chairman of the House Intelligence Committee, Congressman Porter Goss, and the ranking member, Congresswoman Nancy Pelosi. In addition there were a couple of their senior staffers present. We went through each of the specific techniques used in the interrogation of AZ that had been used for a couple of weeks in August. By the time we were briefing the Hill, Abu Zubaydah was compliant and providing good intelligence. We held nothing back and made clear that only authorized techniques, including waterboarding, had been used on Abu Zubaydah.

The interrogation program that was developed was designed to disabuse the detainees of the notion that they were able to control the situation or manipulate us. Each step was designed to drive home to them a sense that their fate was in our hands and that the only way to ensure some semblance of order in their lives was to cooperate. Detainees were brought to a point of cooperation when they concluded that the hopelessness of their situation could end only by cooperating with interrogators. Hopelessness was not defined by pain, but by complete lack of control over one's fate. Detainees were brought to a state of cooperation with the least amount of discomfort because gratuitous pain is counterproductive. The quality of intelligence derived from the process was dependent on the quality of intelligence guiding the debriefer and the skill of the interrogator.

The team came up with a list of thirteen techniques, which was eventually whittled down to ten before the program was implemented. The plan was to use the techniques in a graduated fashion. If a terrorist cooperated with us from the start, none would be employed. If he was nonresponsive, the most benign tactics were used first, and only after the detainee showed that he continued to be noncompliant and after specific written authorization from Agency headquarters would a more aggressive technique be used.

I brought a team of CTC officers to a "Principals Meeting" at the White House at which we described the techniques in some detail. Among those present were the national security advisor, Condoleezza Rice, the attorney general, John Ashcroft, the president's counsel, Alberto Gonzales, and my boss, CIA Director George Tenet. I got the sense from no one that our menu of techniques had gone too far.

The list of enhanced interrogation techniques, known as EITs, had been assembled and was being reviewed by lawyers at the Agency, White House, and Department of Justice. A series of very explicit memos from the Department of Justice laid out exactly what our officers were allowed to do and made clear that in the view of the DOJ none of these steps, when appropriately applied, amounted to torture or any other illegal act. Having seen our officers hung out to dry in the past—for example, during the Iran-Contra period, when differing interpretations of what the law allowed left Agency officers who were doing what their superiors asked vulnerable to results ranging from career suicide to criminal prosecution—I wanted to be sure that we were on solid legal ground. The difficulty was that the program was so closely held that it could not be opened up for a broad public debate.

Years later, the Obama White House authorized the release of many of the underlying documents that revealed the precise language that our officers were operating under. Many critics have inaccurately referred to the legal opinions we received as "the torture memos." In fact they were anything but. Since we specifically asked for guidance to avoid what was illegal under U.S. law—torture—one might say that the DOJ guidance amounted to "nontorture memos." The documents show with extraordinary precision how hard we worked to avoid inflicting lasting harm or pain to our detainees. The documents also reveal something else, something that has gone almost unnoticed. Many of the techniques are essentially bluffs. They were designed to convince the detainees that their situation was considerably more dire than it actually was. For example, one of the techniques that (when described by critics) sounds particularly harsh is "walling." Opponents of our interrogation techniques falsely say that caused detainees' heads to be thrown against walls. In fact the document reveals that special "rooms within rooms" were created with flexible plywood paneling. Interrogators would carefully propel detainees backward so that their shoulder blades would bounce against the plywood, creating a "boom," much like the noise made when professional wrestlers throw each other around the plywood ring without getting hurt. We were after the shock value. In addition to being counterproductive, actually bouncing a detainee's head off a solid wall would be illegal and against what we were all about.

The approval of interrogation techniques came to us in a memo from the Department of Justice's Office of Legal Counsel (OLC). In very precise terms it laid out what actions we could take against Abu Zubaydah. There was never an intent to just unload the entire menu of possible techniques on AZ, or on the handful of other al-Qa'ida terrorists who were later subjected to some of the techniques, nor did we ever do so. Initially, the detainee was jolted by the simple reality that he was now in custody and on totally unfamiliar turf.

Most of the al-Qa'ida detainees in our custody received absolutely no—zero—EITs. The common misconception is that we treated prisoners harshly for months or years on end. The handful who did receive EITs were subjected to them for significantly less time than the authorized thirty days before they became compliant, and then were never subjected to them again.

Arriving detainees had their heads and beards shaved and were given thorough physicals to determine if they had any medical conditions that might make the techniques unsafe for them. CIA officers would then conduct what was basically an entrance interview. This was referred to as a "neutral probe." They simply informed the detainees that they were now in our control and asked if they were willing to cooperate. Some did. If they refused, or cooperated only in a limited way, with head-quarters approval, some subset of the techniques could be used.

Getting "confessions" was generally not a problem. They were proud of what they had done in the past; they just didn't want to talk about attacks that might happen in the future.

Initially, those who refused to cooperate were subjected to "conditioning" techniques. These included sleep deprivation, dietary manipulation, and enforced nudity.

If detainees continued to be unwilling to cooperate, they might receive some of the next level of procedures, which were known as "corrective" techniques. These included things like "the attention grasp," in which the detainee was grabbed on both sides of the collar of his prison garb and in a controlled, quick motion pulled toward the interrogator. Also used was the "facial hold," in which the interrogator would place a hand on each side of the individual's face and hold his head immobile (while taking care to make sure his hands were well away from the detainee's eyes). Finally there was the "insult slap," in which the detainee was slapped somewhere between his chin and the bottom of his earlobe. The interrogators were trained and instructed to make sure their fingers were spread out so that the slap was not particularly painful. The intent was to surprise and humiliate the detainee, not to hurt him. More than one detainee expressed surprise when slapped, and told the interrogator, "Hey, you aren't supposed to do that!" The al-Qa'ida training manual told them that Americans would treat them with kid gloves.

If the detainee still refused to cooperate, then, and only then, would he be subjected to what were called "coercive" techniques. These included being placed in a confined space—essentially a large box in which he could stand up and sit down but in which his movements were physically constrained and uncomfortable, or a smaller box in which there was enough room to sit but not stand. We knew that Abu Zubaydah had an intense fear of bugs, and we were given authority to place a nonbiting, benign insect in the box with him, but the lawyers said that we would have to inform him before doing so that the caterpillar we intended to use was essentially harmless and would not produce severe pain or death. With the psychological sting taken out of this technique, we opted to skip it.

Long before the interrogation techniques became known and the subject of public and media debate, we elected to stop using some of them. Despite the fact that we had been given legal authorization, we simply weren't comfortable with their use and never again employed them.

Another technique that was used from time to time was called "wall standing." The detainee was directed to stand four to five feet from a wall with his arms in front of him and his fingertips resting on the wall. It was intended to produce fatigue but not pain.

Finally, should all else fail, with specific headquarters approval, the detainee might be "waterboarded." The procedure is one that had been safely and widely used for many years in the training of U.S. military personnel. According to the Department of Justice, waterboarding had been used on 26,829 U.S. Air Force personnel between 1992 and 2001. Eventually the air force stopped using the technique, not because it didn't work, and not because they thought it was torture, but because it was *too* effective. The airmen subjected to it found it almost impossible to resist. While the numbers of other service personnel who were subjected to waterboarding is not readily available, it is clear that this was a widely used and understood technique. The navy continued to employ it as part of its SERE training, long after the air force stopped. If it has abandoned the practice, it is likely because of the publicity generated by leaks concerning our interrogation program, rather than concern about the harshness of the technique itself. Since it was so widely used in training of our own military personnel, we were then (and remain now) quite confident that a carefully implemented waterboarding program, such as we envisioned, in no way could accurately be considered "torture."

The description of waterboarding in the DOJ Office of Legal Counsel memo was explicit. It read in part: ". . . the individual is bound securely to an inclined bench, which is approximately four feet by seven feet. The individual's feet are generally elevated. A cloth is placed over the forehead and eyes. Water is then applied to the cloth in a controlled manner. As this is done, the cloth is lowered until it covers both the nose and mouth. Once the cloth is saturated and completely covers the mouth and nose, airflow is slightly restricted for 20 to 40 seconds due to the presence of the cloth. This causes an increase in the carbon dioxide level in the individual's blood. This increase in the carbon dioxide levels stimulates increased effort to breathe. This effort plus the cloth produces the *perception* of 'suffocation and incipient panic' i.e., the *perception* of drowning"(italics mine). Some people argue that because a detainee *thinks* he might be drowning, that makes it torture, whereas military trainees knew that they were in training and could stop the procedure by saying a single word. I'm told that military trainees wonder if their "captors" are going too far and almost immediately come to believe that their situation is dire. Al-Qa'ida detainees also could have ended the session with a single word, a word indicating that they were ready to cooperate. Additionally, KSM was observed counting the seconds off with the fingers of his hand as the waterboarding proceeded, because he knew most applications would last only a few seconds. He quickly figured out that the procedure did not foreshadow imminent death.

The memo went on to say: "The individual does not breathe any water into his lungs. During those 20 to 40 seconds, water is continuously applied from a height of twelve to twenty-four inches. After this period, the cloth is lifted and the individual is allowed to breathe unimpeded for three or four full breaths. The sensation of drowning is immediately relieved by the removal of the cloth. The procedure may then be repeated." Although we were authorized to conduct waterboarding as described above, in fact our officers in the field used far *less* water for far shorter periods of time than they were allowed.

Unfortunately, once the matter of waterboarding became generally known, the public was only given (quite literally) a cartoon version of what others imagine the technique was like. Irresponsible animations showed detainees practically being dowsed by a fire hose.

The EITs were employed by our officers with great reluctance and solemnity. No one enjoyed doing it, but we were absolutely convinced that people like AZ had information in their heads that would save countless American lives. We were right.

Once Abu Zubaydah broke under waterboarding, he told our officers something remarkable. "You must do this for all the brothers," he said. AZ explained to them that Allah knew that they were only human and once they had been tested to their limits there was no shame in their cooperating with us. He understood why we were doing what we were doing and explained that when al-Qa'ida got their hands on their enemies, and especially when they caught one of their own members who they thought was a spy, their treatment was infinitely harsher.

Once he became compliant, the information AZ willingly provided us was by any reasonable measure some of the most important intelligence collected since 9/11. Those who say otherwise are simply ill informed or misleading the public.

Chapter 4

KHALID SHEIKH MOHAMMED

For those working in the CIA's Counterterrorism Center, the first six months of the post-9/11 world was a blur. There wasn't time to grieve over the loss of thousands of our countrymen, a loss that, despite great effort, the Agency and our counterparts throughout government had failed to prevent. Every ounce of our energy had to be poured into the response. As I have said, while the awful hours of September 11 were inarguably the worst in the CIA's history, I believe the days that followed were our best.

In some ways I was like many of my new colleagues. I was performing in a job that days before did not exist. Our ultimate goal was clear, but the path to it was not. Countless new people poured into CTC, and many were crammed into a maze of cubicles so confusing we had to hang cardboard street signs above the narrow aisles so that officers could find their counterparts. "Want to see Jim? Sure, take a right on Usama Bin Lane and it is the third cubicle on the left. If you get to Zawahiri Way you've gone too far."

The war against terrorists was being fought on many fronts, but none was more important in the near term than the one in Afghanistan. A CTC veteran by the name of Hank Crumpton was brought back from an overseas assignment, at which he had just arrived, and at considerable sacrifice for him and his family, to orchestrate the efforts to roust al-Qa'ida from its comfortable lair in Afghanistan and drive its Taliban protectors from power. The plan was not just a CIA plan. It was so well conceived that it became the nation's plan. A relative handful of CIA officers, in concert with a couple of hundred special operations forces troops, worked miracles. The story of how that plan was formulated and implemented is a remarkable one, but it is one that has been well told in books such as George Tenet's memoir and Hank Crumpton's soon-to-be released *The Art of Intelligence,* and I won't devote much space to it here. As the plan was being built and carried out, Cofer Black, CTC's leader, was jetting around the world building partnerships with allies and former foes alike to capitalize on the near-universal revulsion at what al-Qa'ida had done and to enlist new partners in the fight against them and their associates. Cofer's deputy, Ben Bonk, a soft-spoken, gentle, and insightful analyst, was spending countless hours in meetings at the White House with DOD, State Department, and other interagency colleagues trying to maintain focus on the critical task at hand.

With CTC's two top leaders fully consumed, I focused on keeping our rapidly growing organization on track. I made it a priority to keep the Agency's top leadership (collectively known as the "seventh floor") informed of what CTC was doing and taking guidance from them and passing it along to our troops. After a short period of complete cooperation post-9/11, as time passed there were occasionally ruffled feathers within other parts of the CIA that suddenly found themselves on the losing end of personnel, space, money, and responsibility realignments. I tried hard to patch up any hard feelings and to get everyone to feel as though they were part of a great team effort, which they were.

Operationally, things were going pretty well. Cooperation from international partners was at an all-time high. The Taliban had been routed. Al-Qa'ida was spending most of its efforts to preserve its own existence and therefore had less time to spend trying to end ours. Yet our increased intelligence-collection capabilities produced a continuing flood of threat information. Working in conjunction with the FBI, CTC was producing a product called the "Threat Matrix," which went to the president and other senior leaders, cataloguing the latest threats to come in over the transom. Many of the threats were cataclysmic in nature. We knew that most of them were bogus; we just didn't know which ones.

It is impossible to overstate the stress our officers were under. Every sign pointed to the fact that al-Qa'ida was planning another wave of attacks, and we were convinced then and remain convinced today that they hoped to exceed the devastation of 9/11 with the next wave. The so-called chatter picked up from intercepted communications was just one of the indicators we had to go on. There were other even more ominous signs.

Among the material found at the time of Abu Zubaydah's capture were videotapes he had prepared in advance to celebrate another yet-to-happen al-Qa'ida success. The tapes were designed to rally supporters and solicit funds from backers of their evil jihad. At least one of them suggested that Abu Zubaydah had been to Iran or was somehow cooperating with the Iranians. Surely Abu Zubaydah would not have gone to the trouble of making these tapes unless they had some very specific and sizable plans in mind. But what were those plans?

The months of continuous stress were taking their toll on CTC officers. Despite working twelve-, fifteen-, or eighteen-hour days, the common feeling as they made the long trek to the CIA headquarters parking lot was: "Maybe if I stay just one more hour, pore over a few more documents, listen to a handful more intercepts, I can find the key that will prevent another attack."

As stressful as the lives of CTC personnel back in Langley were, that was nothing compared to the burden on officers on the front lines in Afghanistan, Pakistan, and hellholes around the world.

I struggled constantly to remind our young officers that they should not neglect their families or their health. This was going to be a long fight, and we would not be able to win it if our key people burned themselves out chasing our foes to the point that the CIA officers dropped from exhaustion.

In early May 2002 I was in for a couple of big shocks. First I was told that our boss, Cofer Black, was leaving CTC. Battered from doing battle with al-Qa'ida and sometimes against U.S. and allied bureaucracy, Cofer was going to spend some time helping the Agency prepare for the inevitable outside investigations about how 9/11 could have happened. Later he would go on to become an ambassadorial-level counterterrorism coordinator at the Department of State.

The second surprise was even bigger. I was asked to replace Cofer. Eight months before, the Agency's Directorate of Operations was unsure if they had a job for me, and now I was being asked to take on their biggest mission imaginable.

I didn't have a lot of time to spend wondering why George Tenet had selected me for the job. To many insiders, I am sure, it was quite a surprise. A guy named Jose Rodriguez who spent most of his professional career running operations in Latin America and with only modest experience in counterterrorism was being thrust into a job in which you might expect to find the most seasoned Arabic-speaking Middle East hand.

Looking back, I suspect the fact that I had run large stations and multidiscipline organizations for the Agency and my reputation for being someone who built strong teams were part of the rationale. Whatever the reason, the turnover was swift, and before I could think twice, I found myself with a tremendous challenge on my plate. I was certain (incorrectly as it turned out) that this would be my final assignment as an Agency officer and I desperately wanted it to be a success.

At one point, the director took me to the White House to

meet with the president for a Saturday "deep dive" on coun-terterrorism. The president had obviously been briefed on my background and knew that my last field assignment had been in Mexico. An engaging and personal man in private, he wanted to chat with me about my experience there in Spanish. He rattled off something that I couldn't quite get. *"Cómo?"* I asked. He said it again and it was just as unintelligible to me. How odd, I thought, that my career might go down in flames over my in-ability to understand the president's Spanish. Finally, with great difficulty, I figured out he was asking about a politician who was running for president of Mexico. To my relief, I was right.

My transition to chief of CTC came during a precarious time. We had just captured our first major al-Qa'ida figure, Abu Zubaydah, and were struggling to figure out how to make the best use of the critical information we were getting out of him before the next wave of attacks might cross our shores.

In the nine months since September 11, we had grown enormously in personnel, resources, and authorities. I had some extraordinarily able leaders working under me who were seized with the importance of our mission. I knew that I needed to empower them, inspire them, and prevent well-meaning but cumbersome government bureaucrats from get-ting in their way. I recognized that while we had been very successful during the Afghan phase of the war, we would have to adjust to be able to handle what was to come next. I gave orders that the compartmentalization that was typical of almost all intelligence organizations at the time must end in CTC. Our analysts were given access to the most sensitive operational databases. It may seem odd to outsiders, but in the intelligence community we spend a lot of time keeping secrets from each other. While there are security reasons for doing so, it can im-pede successful operations. We took a risk to share information more widely in CTC, and I never regretted my decision.

Another of my priorities was to improve coordination not just with the Agency's leadership on the seventh floor but also with the intelligence community, Congress, and the White House. All these organizations were bombarding CTC with requests for information, many of which could not be answered in a timely manner without getting in the way of critical operations. I wanted my people to pound away at the operational target, and my job was to get them the resources and people they needed. I also spent a lot of my time meeting and developing close relationships with our liaison partners by visiting them overseas and meeting them in Washington.

One of the best things about working at the CIA is how "flat" an organization it is. The number of layers between an operative in the field and the head of CTC, for example, is remarkably few. Decisions can be made much more quickly and with far fewer sign-offs than would be found in the military or in most major corporations.

The information coming out of Abu Zubaydah's debriefing proved to be extraordinarily valuable. Things that were learned from his questioning at the black site were shared almost instantly with analysts and operators back at headquarters. Taking the threads of information he was providing us and weaving them into a fuller context, we were able to launch operations within a matter of hours or days that led to the capture, killing, or disrupting of many other al-Qa'ida operatives.

One of the many myths about our enhanced interrogation program is that the harsh treatment continued during the entire time we held the senior detainees. In fact, only a handful of the most knowledgeable detainees received any rough treatment and in those cases, the techniques were permanently halted once the detainee became compliant. In Abu Zubaydah's case, he moved from the interrogation to the debriefing stage quickly. It was less than a month after the enhanced interrogation techniques started in August 2002 when they ended for him.

Once AZ became compliant the harsh treatment stopped and we began questioning him. He quickly impressed our officers with his intelligence, depth of knowledge, and willingness to help. As one officer later told me, "He became part of our team." That doesn't mean that we blindly accepted what he had to say. Every statement he made was checked and double-checked. Far more often than not, however, he told us the truth.

CIA officers at the black site developed an odd affection for him. A woman officer who was assigned to the debriefing team described him to me as a "mensch." "He loves his mother," she said, "and tried hard to take care of his al-Qa'ida brothers." AZ was responsible for finding wives for some of the al-Qa'ida operatives and at one point even "gave away" a potential wife of his own to take care of the needs of one of his charges.

And yet, despite his part-time charisma and cooperative spirit, Abu Zubaydah was no innocent. His prime motivation was his hatred for Jews. He was deeply devoted to the Palestinian cause and expressed great unhappiness that bin Ladin and others elected to launch their devastating 9/11 attack on the United States, whereas he would have much preferred that the target have been Israel.

During one conversation in which AZ was showing the softer side of his personality, one of his debriefers tossed out a hypothetical question. "If you were made free today, what would you do?" she asked. Without hesitation AZ answered: "Rejoin the jihad and kill Jews."

Such comments were stark reminders that despite the fact that some of the detainees would occasionally display normal human tendencies, there was a very good reason for us to imprison them and to plumb the depths of the plots that they and others had hatched.

When it became clear that the EITs worked and that we were going to be accumulating a number of additional senior al-Qa'ida operatives who might be candidates for them, I ordered some of my staff to create a training program so that additional officers could learn precisely how they were to apply the techniques. The course lasted two weeks. Those going through it were carefully screened by Agency psychologists before they were allowed to enter the program, and a couple of volunteers were not selected to participate because of that review. The careful and precise application of the techniques, carried out by people who were themselves psychologically equipped to administer them, was something we insisted on.

The debriefing of Abu Zubaydah following the use of the EITs paid immediate dividends. Information he provided led to the capture of Ramzi bin al-Shibh in a gun battle in Karachi, which happened to take place on September 11, 2002. Bin al-Shibh had been part of al-Qa'ida's "Hamburg cell" and was a close associate of at least three of the 9/11 hijackers. He had intended to be part of that operation. He was not only because he could not get a valid U.S. visa to enter the United States.

Bin al-Shibh consoled himself with the role of communications coordinator for al-Qa'ida with the hijackers who did make it into the U.S. He never lost his zeal for murder, however. A few months after 9/11 we captured five martyrdom videos, including one of bin al-Shibh vowing to commit suicide for the cause.

In the same raid that produced Ramzi bin al-Shibh's capture, we were able to nab several other important al-Qa'ida players and capture a lot of very valuable documentation. One of the operatives seemed to have been somewhat obsessive-compulsive and had amassed a huge stockpile of receipts and a variety of other documents that were a windfall for our analysts. Also found at the site was a spare prosthetic leg belonging to AQ operative Walid bin Attash. Sadly, bin Attash wasn't connected to it at the time. Some of our people discovered that bin Attash had frequented online dating websites and described himself as someone who "Loves to travel—sometimes at a moment's notice." It took us six more months, but finally we captured him in Karachi in April 2003 and put a serious dent in his social life.

AZ's debriefing led directly to the arrest and detention of a number of other al-Qa'ida supporters, some of whom ended up residing with him at our black site. One particularly disreputable example was Abd al-Rahim al-Nashiri, who was captured in the fall of 2002. Al-Nashiri was the self-proclaimed "mastermind" of the bombing of the USS *Cole* on October 12, 2000, while the ship was at anchor in Aden, killing seventeen U.S. Navy sailors and very nearly sinking the $250 million warship.

"Mastermind" was not an apt description of al-Nashiri. One of our interrogators described him to me as "the dumbest terrorist I have ever met." He was also one of the vilest. It is impossible to describe this gently, but al-Nashiri was a nose picker who delighted in plastering the wall of his cell with whatever he could excavate from his nostrils. He also enjoyed throwing food around his cell and refused to clean up his mess.

Abu Zubaydah suggested a way of dealing with al-Nashiri's disgusting habits. "Drag me into his cell," he said, "and throw me onto the floor. Don't be gentle about it. Order me to clean up my brother's mess. He will be ashamed and change his habits."

The scenario played out just as he had scripted it. Al-Nashiri was quick to pull AZ away from his cleanup chores and to promise that he would not put him in that position again.

We learned a lot from Abu Zubaydah, and not just the intelligence we collected. He also essentially gave us the playbook we used to get the most information out of fellow top operatives, people like Khalid Sheikh Mohammed.

We were convinced that al-Nashiri was in a position to know about impending attacks, and he was subjected to EITs. He was the second person to undergo waterboarding, but unlike AZ he became compliant almost immediately.

For the most part, al-Nashiri's interrogation went by the book. There were a few exceptions. In one case, two CIA officers blew cigar smoke in his face. Not particularly cruel treatment, but as an example of how carefully the approved steps were being monitored, those officers were reported to their Agency superiors for exceeding authorized guidelines.

Subsequently al-Nashiri told us the next al-Qa'ida attack might come in housing compounds in Saudi Arabia. We immediately notified our Saudi counterparts, but al-Nashiri insisted that he didn't have any additional information. About six months later, on May 12, 2003, a group of heavily armed terrorists in an SUV, a pickup truck, and two cars stormed a housing compound in Riyadh, killing thirty-one people, including nine American citizens.

In addition to being dumb, al-Nashiri was heartless. He was asked why his operatives who conducted the suicide attack on the USS *Cole* were not allowed to try to save themselves before their explosive-laden boat detonated against the hull of the American destroyer, killing seventeen U.S. sailors and injuring thirty-nine others, and nearly sinking the ship. Al-Nashiri just shrugged. Their survival didn't matter, he said.

With each new detainee we gained new insights into what they were likely to know and what actions were best to get the latest arrivals to cooperate. Our officers weren't above a little theatrics. There was one case, which was later dubbed "Operation Kebab," in which a new detainee who was being fed a reduced-calorie, but medically healthy, diet was moved in shackles from one part of the building to another. He and his escorts happened to pass through another room where a fellow detainee (who had already become compliant) was enjoying a large, sumptuous meal. His captors told him something funny just before the reluctant detainee came by. The shackled prisoner saw his unchained former colleague laughing uproariously and chowing down with gusto. The ruse worked. "That's it," the detainee said. "My jihad is over." He was ready for serious talk—and kebab.

One of the many myths about interrogating terrorists is the "all or nothing" fable. Some people suggest that captured terrorists will tell you nothing unless and until you squeeze them, at which point they will tell you everything. That is far from the case. Often they will tell you things they think are trivial or will provide information that they mistakenly think you already know. Such was the case in the early days of Abu Zubaydah's interrogation, long before he was subjected to enhanced interrogation techniques, when he solved a mystery for us.

For years we had been seeing in intelligence traffic references to a high-ranking al-Qa'ida official who was known by the alias "Mukhtar." We knew this person was heavily involved in a wide range of past AQ plots and figured that he was likely in on future plans as well. Al-Qa'ida uses lots of pseudonyms in its communications, and many operatives use similar or matching names, so it is only through the context that recipients of email and telephonic communications know whom they are talking about. So we were delighted when Abu Zubaydah let slip the true identity of "Mukhtar." A cable back to CIA headquarters put it simply:

"Mukhtar = KSM."

Khalid Sheikh Mohammed had also been known to the intelligence community for many years, but we did not know the full extent of his role in al-Qa'ida. We later learned that he had up to fifty aliases and that if there was a single person who deserved the awful title of "mastermind" of the 9/11 plot, it was KSM.

As I previously described, the information gleaned from Abu Zubaydah, particularly after the application of the EITs, provided a road map to identifying, locating, and capturing a string of top al-Qa'ida operatives. Based on complex link analysis, we were able to learn which terrorist associated with which other AQ members, how they communicated, and how they supported each other. As a result, we were able to lay meticulous plans that we hoped would lead us to the biggest catches.

We got close to KSM a couple of times. At one point we had narrowed down his whereabouts to a few square miles in Karachi. But a few square miles in that crowded city can host tens of thousands of people. Working with Pakistani liaison, we tried to narrow it down. But then a corrupt Pakistani policeman who had somehow learned of the effort tipped off KSM. An email from the crooked cop was intercepted. In it he told KSM, "They know where you are." That was good news and bad news. Good, because it helped us pinpoint KSM's location, but bad because it took us a couple of days coordinating with Pakistani officials to orchestrate a raid. By the time we got there, KSM was gone. We found videotapes, documents, children's clothing that belonged to his kids, and other evidence that we had just missed our target. In the trash, written in English in red ink, was information about the murder of American journalist Danny Pearl. After getting so close to being captured, KSM stopped using cell phones and email in an effort to hide his trail.

At one point, in a location I can't describe, the Agency met with a man who said he had contacts that might lead us to KSM. This guy had at least two motivations. He was not happy about the way his religion had been hijacked by al-Qa'ida. He thought that the terrorists had done tremendous damage to the image of Islam. But he was also interested in the hefty financial rewards the CIA was offering for those who could help us get to senior AQ leaders. He said he was interested in becoming our "agent." You often hear the media describe people like me and my colleagues as "CIA agents." In CIA parlance, we call our employees "officers." Those who conduct clandestine operations are generally "case officers." The foreign nationals whom we recruit to spy on our behalf are termed "agents." If you hear Americans call themselves a "CIA agent" or "former agent," you can almost automatically assume they are fakes.

Our officers on the scene wanted to test this volunteer with some low-level projects to see if he was able to deliver. But he was not interested in starting small. I guess he figured that if he was to take the risk of betraying any al-Qa'ida figures, he might as well make the reward involved worthwhile.

Our agent contacted his CIA handlers and said that he might be able to lead us to KSM.

I am not able to describe what happened next in full detail, but here is a brief description—with some facts fuzzed up to protect lives.

Our agent told us he had been invited to meet with a group of people, one of whom might be in contact with KSM. We staked out an internet café where the meeting was to take place. We didn't know what the person we were targeting looked like. So a signal had been agreed upon. If the person who was believed to be in contact with KSM was among the group, our agent was told to put his hat on as he left the building. If the target was not among the group, he should walk out carrying his hat. It seemed like a simple plan. What we didn't count on was that there would be a torrential downpour just as our agent was leaving the café. True to his training, he calmly strolled outside with hat in hand, getting drenched in the process. It was disappointing to learn that the KSM contact wasn't there, but this kind of work requires great patience.

When our agent left, however, we noticed that he got into a car with others from the group. It seemed too dangerous to follow them. Al-Qa'ida countersurveillance would almost certainly have picked up our team and have been alerted. So our officers let the agent disappear into the teeming suburbs and waited for news.

They waited and waited. Finally, the CIA officers on the scene did what workers do everywhere at the end of a long day: They adjourned to happy hour. While enjoying a few drinks, one of the Agency officers got a text message from our agent, who said, "I can get you to KSM." "Holy shit," he said. They threw a bunch of money on the table and sprinted out of the place, demonstrating understandable enthusiasm but perhaps not the best of stealthy tradecraft.

Agency officers rendezvoused with our agent, who told them he had a pretty good idea where KSM was staying in Rawalpindi, Pakistan's third-largest city, with close to four million inhabitants. It practically abuts the nation's capital, Islamabad, and is home to the headquarters of the Pakistani armed forces.

Our officers rushed to the scene with thirty pieces of body armor.

A joint Pakistani and American team stormed the home where KSM was staying shortly after midnight on March 1, 2003. KSM grabbed an AK-47. Unlike Saddam Hussein, Usama bin Ladin, and Muammar Qadhafi, who were cornered long after him, KSM managed to get off a few shots. He wounded a Pakistani officer before being captured.

A CIA officer snapped the now-famous image of a disheveled KSM moments after the capture. As is so often the case, word of the operation leaked almost immediately. In the aftermath of the capture, several media outlets romanticized KSM's role in al-Qa'ida, some even referring to him as the "James Bond" of al-Qa'ida. To counter that impression, the CIA released the iconic photo of KSM looking much more like John Belushi than Agent 007.

The Pakistanis took KSM to a safe-house holding facility while the details of his ultimate disposition were worked out. We immediately began exploiting the mother lode of information that had been found in the home where he had been staying. The first few hours and days following a capture like this one are critical. The value of material found around a detainee diminishes as time passes and fellow al-Qa'ida members who were not captured have time to do damage control.

In the immediate aftermath of KSM's capture we learned that he had told people that he had met with Ayman al-Zawahiri, bin Ladin's deputy, a few days before. If true, that meant Zawahiri was likely nearby. Even more enticing just before his capture, KSM flashed a note that he said had been given to him by bin Ladin himself. KSM told people he had been asked to get the note to one of bin Ladin's sons telling him to stay off the internet. Much later KSM claimed that he was just bragging and had written the note himself. Our officers were not so sure. Back in early March 2003, the fact that KSM might have been in recent contact with UBL only heightened our desire to quickly get whatever information we could from him.

We had CIA officers take turns sitting with KSM in the initial hours at the safe house. We were worried that left to the Pakistanis alone, he might make some miraculous escape, aided by officials who were more philosophically aligned with AQ's goals than with those of the U.S.A.

Getting our officers into the safe house without attracting attention was not an easy thing. One of our guys later told me of being put into the back of a pickup truck and told to lie down under a tarp so that he would not be seen by nearby guards. It occurred to him as he was being spirited toward the safe house that he was putting an awful lot of trust in his Pakistani colleagues. He could hear the driver shouting in Urdu, one of the principal languages of Pakistan, but he couldn't make out what was being said. Eventually they got to the small building, a foul-smelling place with three guards, only one of whom seemed to have a weapon. That guard didn't inspire much confidence either. He waved the weapon around recklessly, using it as a pointing tool and demonstrating none of the "muzzle security" that Americans like to see as a factor in promoting longevity.

Our officers tried to start the interrogation process right then and there, but with scant success. They had six-hour shifts with our prize catch, who was not in a talkative mood. KSM elected to incessantly chant Koranic verses and ignore the questions from CIA officers. The Pakistanis had a presence in the room at times, too. Periodically, an officer would run into the room and shout, "Where is bin Ladin?" KSM would ignore him and he would leave.

At one point a very large major took a shot at questioning, or more accurately screaming at, KSM. He sat on a small desk in the holding room, which immediately collapsed. KSM started laughing and said in Urdu, "That's what you get for working with dogs."

It was clear he didn't have much else he wanted to say. Finally, after trying to question him without success for a day, our people on the scene decided to let him earn a chance to go to sleep. Our officer made KSM stand up, which required some assistance. At five-foot-three and considerably overweight, to our guy, KSM felt "gooey" as he was helped to his feet.

"Here's the deal, Mukhtar," he said. "I know you speak English" (KSM graduated from college in North Carolina in

1986). "I want you to politely ask me to let you go to sleep. Do that and I will let you." The idea was to demonstrate to KSM that he was no longer in control. KSM stood there mute for twenty minutes. Finally he mumbled something in Urdu. Our officer said, "You have to ask in English." More silence. About five minutes later KSM mumbled something else. "What was that?" he was asked. A weak voice said: "May I sleep?" The CIA officer shouted, "What? What did you say?" KSM wearily but more loudly said, "May I sleep?" "Yes, yes you can," he was told by the CIA officer, who was in desperate need of rest himself.

After a night's sleep our officers tried once again to get KSM to talk. While he gave up pretending to speak only Urdu, he didn't give up much else. When it came time for the officer who had granted KSM permission to sleep the night before to have another turn watching the portly prisoner, Mohammed surprised him by asking: "Will you be nice to me?" It was not exactly what he had expected to hear. "What do you mean?" he asked. "Are you going to yell at me?" KSM asked. "If I yelled at you last night, it was because I was frustrated," the Agency officer replied. KSM held out his beefy paw and shook the officer's hand.

KSM started to engage a little. Like other AQ officials, he would talk a bit about past deeds but would say nothing about future plans. He was asked about the location of bin Ladin and Zawahiri and how al-Qa'ida communicated with them. KSM remained silent. He was asked what operations the group was planning. KSM looked directly in the eyes of his inquisitor and simply said: "Soon you will know." It so happened that the officer in the cell with him had previously worked trying to find out who had brutally murdered *Wall Street Journal* reporter Danny Pearl. Since a document relating to Pearl had previously been found at the home where KSM was staying, our officer asked Mohammed to tell him about his involvement in the reporter's death. KSM wagged his finger at the American, paused, and then cryptically said: "Not now."

Within a few days we were able to spirit KSM out of Pakistan and take him to a black site. There the process began with him, just as it had with other recent senior detainees, to try to get him to voluntarily share the information we knew he had. From material found at the location of his capture we had indications that he had had recent contact with bin Ladin and Zawahiri. From other detainees we knew that he was instrumental in coming up with the plans that led to 9/11. And from his own words when we asked what al-Qa'ida planned next we had his haunting words: "Soon you will know." With all that, we couldn't idly sit by and wait for a chance to bond with our detainee or for him to see the error of his ways and open up to us. So, after he refused to cooperate, the EITs were methodically implemented one by one in an effort to stave off another horrific attack on the United States or one of our allies.

Some detainees agreed to cooperate after little more than a stern look. Others took a bit more convincing but would become compliant after a relatively small dose of EITs. And then there was KSM. Agency officers in charge of his detention described him as "pure evil." He was very strong-minded and gave every sign of having had considerable training in how to resist interrogation. Even the most severe technique, waterboarding, which was employed on him and only two other detainees, did not produce immediate results. KSM seemed to have figured out that we weren't going to push things too far. While strapped down on a gurney and as water was being applied, he used his fingers to tick off the seconds. What eventually brought KSM to the compliant stage was more sleep deprivation. Finally, when he reached his limit, he decided that continued resistance was unwise and he began to cooperate. That doesn't mean that he told us everything he knew. And it doesn't mean that he told us what we wanted most. But he did begin to open up and fill in many, many blanks in our knowledge of al-Qa'ida.

As with the others, once KSM reached the compliant stage, the EITs stopped. We moved from the "interrogation" phase to the "debriefing" mode. Agency officers on scene had long before figured out that KSM had an enormous ego, and they played on it to our advantage. He enjoyed thinking of himself as a professor. He leaped at the chance to show off his knowledge.

The information he provided was enormously helpful in understanding our foe and finding ways to thwart their plans. It is important to stress that we never took anything he said on faith but always vetted it in every way possible. Many of those listening were in fact among the most knowledgeable people on the planet about the organization and membership of al-Qa'ida and could spot it when KSM might be trying to lead them astray or shade the truth.

The information that came from KSM, like that from Abu Zubaydah before him, was a treasure trove. A study by NBC News in 2008 showed that 441 of the 1,700 footnotes in the 9/11 Commission's final report came from senior al-Qa'ida detainee interrogation. The percentage of information that came from them in Chapters 5, 6, and 7 of the report, the portions dealing directly with the 9/11 plot, were well over 50 percent from the interrogations.

The windfall reported in the intelligence reports coming out of KSM's interrogation was so dramatic that FBI officials petitioned the CIA to get back into the interrogation program, which they had abandoned during the early days at the first black site. At the time they said they didn't want to be party to enhanced interrogation. Now they wanted back in. Agency leadership said no. In part we were afraid that FBI special agents would only disrupt the program. But another factor was that the location of the new sites was not known to them and we didn't want to expand the circle of witting officials for fear that knowledge of the sites would leak and their effectiveness would be compromised if not ended.

Even though in their eyes, KSM remained one of the most evil persons in the world, CIA officers at the black site established a strange symbiotic relationship with him and an oddly cordial rapport. KSM told one of our most senior women debriefers that he much preferred dealing with CIA women; he found them better prepared and less judgmental. He told the male debriefers something different, telling one that he was glad to see that the CIA wasn't entirely run by women.

At the end of one debriefing session, the CIA officer who was questioning KSM got up to leave. He called her back and said, "There is something else you should know." He proceeded to tell her how he had personally decapitated *Wall Street Journal* reporter Daniel Pearl in early 2002. KSM spoke of the atrocity in a matter-of-fact tone. He provided considerable detail to back up his claim and clearly was not at all remorseful.

The report of his confession rocketed back to Washington. There were many of us who were prepared to believe any evil deed was well within KSM's capacity. Some had had suspicions about his involvement ever since documents found in Pakistan seemed to connect him to the murder. Others thought, however, that it might just be a ploy. One of KSM's frequently stated goals was to be put on trial in New York. Shortly after he was captured he told Agency officers that he would talk only after he got to New York and met with his lawyer. It seemed to us that he was looking for a platform from which he could spout his hatred for all things American, and a trial would certainly present that opportunity. (It strikes me as more than a little ironic that several years later Attorney General Eric Holder almost granted KSM his wish.)

Back at CIA headquarters, analysts scrutinized once again the grisly videotape of Pearl's murder. Although the face of the person wielding the knife was covered, the person's hand, shown as he killed the reporter, did resemble KSM's. Closer examination of the video was required to study Pearl's execu- tioner. Analysts in Washington asked that close-up photos of KSM's hand and arm be taken while he was holding a sack with a bowling ball in it to simulate the severed head held in the gruesome video. Those photos compared to the actual video showed that KSM was not lying to us. In a confession he later submitted for a potential tribunal in Guantanamo Bay, Cuba, KSM wrote: "I decapitated with blessed right hand the head of the American Jew, Daniel Pearl, in the city of Karachi, Pakistan," adding, "For those who would like to confirm, there are pictures of me on the internet holding his head."

One debriefer later told me that she viewed KSM as the al-Qa'ida Hannibal Lecter. And yet, as odd as it sounds, he had a playful side, too. On several occasions he wrote letters to register complaints about his living conditions. In one, he wrote as if he were writing to his congressman. In another he penned a letter of complaint to the electric company objecting to the chilliness in his cell. This was well after the short period of less than two weeks when he was subjected to EITs. "Unless you are trying to manipulate me," he wrote, "could you turn up the heat a bit?" He also wrote notes complaining that a guard had allegedly taken a bite out of an apple on his food tray. Just another example of our brutal treatment, I guess.

Although he could appear gregarious at times, we knew that he had been quite standoffish when he attended college in Greensboro, North Carolina. When asked why, he said it was because the United States had too many homosexuals and he didn't want to associate with them.

Despite the popular misconception that Agency officers treated KSM cruelly during the three-plus years he was in our custody, the harsh treatment, which I believe to have been "necessary roughness," lasted for only days. Later, CIA officers engaged with him on a familiar basis and actually joined KSM in his cell on occasion to watch movies—complete with popcorn. To avoid inflaming any sensitivities, movies shared with detainees were carefully selected and usually PG-rated at most.

But no one was taken in by his moments of normalcy. At one point he was told that if he provided some vital additional information we would facilitate communication between him and his two children. "I don't care," he said, "they are in Allah's hands."

KSM enjoyed lecturing CIA officers, individually and in groups. At one point he announced that he would like to give a lecture on "The History of the World." Our folks were game and went to hear him expound on that ambitious topic. A few months later he reported that he was ready to continue and build on his earlier presentation. He had one requirement, however. Only those officers who had sat through the prerequisite first session (History of the World 101, so to speak) should be invited to attend the 201 session.

One of our senior CTC officers spent some time at the black site and established what seemed to have been a good relationship with KSM, getting some very valuable information from him. His contact with KSM came long after the "difficult period" (as the detainees called it) when EITs were employed. When it was time for this officer to return to headquarters, he dropped by KSM's cell to say good-bye. Mohammed surprised him by saying: "Have a safe trip." Sensing that what he had just said might be taken as a sign of humanity, KSM quickly added:

"It is not that I wish you well. But if I ever get out of here, I want to personally be the one to kill you."

Beyond his hope for being brought to trial in New York, KSM also speculated that he might be given the opportunity to testify before Congress someday. One CIA officer who heard that aspiration told him, "You don't understand our government very well."

In many respects the CIA officer was right, but at least two of our people at the black site told me that KSM made an observation to them that would later prove eerily accurate. Talking about his interrogation and that of his colleagues, he said: "You know, someday your government is going to turn on you."

Chapter 5

TAKING PRISONERS

Once KSM became compliant and started cooperating with his debriefers, which was within a month of his capture, he became the gift that kept on giving. KSM and the other senior detainees in our custody provided a wealth of information. Of all the other tools in the U.S. intelligence arsenal, none provided the quantity or quality of critical information that we got from this handful of al-Qa'ida operatives.

That is not to say that they told us everything they knew. But they provided good, actionable intelligence leads of incredible value. Each success seemed to lead to another. Often when a detainee learned that we had picked up one of his former colleagues, he assumed that the other person would be cooperating with us. We leveraged one against the other. We would go to a new arrival and say "KSM has told us all about you," and provide a nugget from our files. That person, believing there was little left to hide, would provide new details, which we would take back to KSM.

For example, at about the same time that KSM was captured, we nabbed another al-Qa'ida operative by the name of Majid Khan in Pakistan. Khan was a onetime resident of Baltimore, Maryland, and, according to some accounts, had been training in Pakistan to learn how to blow up gas stations, poison water supplies, and even possibly attempt an assassination of Pakistani president Musharraf.

While being debriefed, KSM told us that he had used Majid Khan to deliver fifty thousand dollars to a major AQ operative in Southeast Asia, Riduan Isamuddin, who went by the nom de guerre Hambali.

Our officers confronted Khan with this information and he essentially confirmed KSM's story, with a slight twist. He said he had passed the money on via a Malaysian man called Zubair, and he even remembered his phone number. Armed with that, we soon had Zubair in custody. His true name is Mohamad Farik Amin. Before long Zubair was cooperating, too, and he provided information that led to the capture of another top Hambali aide, by the name of Bashir bin Lap, who was also known as Lillie.

Lillie in turn provided the information that was used to capture Hambali in Thailand. Second perhaps only to KSM, Hambali was one of the most significant takedowns of al-Qa'ida leaders we were able to conduct. Hambali had worked with KSM in 1995 planning "Operation Bojinka," a plot intended to simultaneously blow up a dozen airliners flying from Asia to the United States. Although that plot was narrowly thwarted, not all of Hambali's efforts failed. In 2002 he was the mastermind behind the bombing of a nightclub in Bali in which almost two hundred people were killed.

Hambali was important for many reasons. He was a high-level al-Qa'ida operative but also a leader of the Jemaah Islamiyah terrorist group. At a time when much of the world was alert to the possibility of Arab terrorists, Hambali led a group of Asians who had a better chance of getting close to their targets without detection. We were very worried that if we focused too much on Arab terrorists we would be hammered by an al-Qa'ida affiliate with different ethnicity.

Once we had Hambali in custody, Agency officers went back to KSM and asked him to answer a hypothetical question: "If Hambali were no longer around, who was likely to take his place in Southeast Asia?" KSM said that was an easy one. If Hambali were not around, the slot almost certainly would be filled by Hambali's brother, Rusman Gunawan, who went by the apt nickname Gun Gun.

Our debriefers chatted with Hambali about his background and family. Without knowing what he was doing, he inadvertently provided information that allowed us to track down his brother in Pakistan and to orchestrate moving Gun Gun into custody at a black site, too.

Gun Gun in turn told us about a seventeen-member Jemaah Islamiyah group, known as the Guraba cell, which was in Karachi preparing for future terrorist attacks. The members of the group were South Asians. At a time when the world was focused on looking for young Arab men, al-Qa'ida tried to change the face of terrorism. Soon the Guraba cell was also rolled up. We believe this group would have been used for a planned second-wave airline attack on the U.S. West Coast similar to the 9/11 attacks.

So if you have followed the tale above, you can clearly see that information we got from detainees, some of whom talked only after being subjected to enhanced interrogation techniques, provided huge dividends. Those critics who say, "These guys would tell you anything to get the harsh treatment to stop" fail to understand that any harsh treatment stopped long before the information was provided. Even more important, no matter what a detainee told us, we would not accept it on blind faith but checked it out in many different ways.

Information from AZ, KSM, and the others led to the capture of a large number of other al-Qa'ida operatives and the probable disruption of many potential plots. Skeptics often ask, "Exactly how many plots did you stop?" When we can't give them a precise number they assume the number is low. But often when we learned of a particular AQ focus on a potential target, we would get word to the appropriate officials to beef up security at that location, making the area too hot for AQ operatives to function nearby. Can I tell you exactly how many plots were stopped? No. But I am confident that more than ten serious mass-casualty attacks were thwarted because of information received from detainees who had been subjected to enhanced interrogation, and it is much better to stop plots while they are in the planning stage than just before execution.

Just a few weeks after KSM's capture, Iyman Faris, a Pakistani-American with a hazardous-materials truck-driving license who lived in Ohio, was arrested. KSM told us that he had dispatched Faris to survey suspension bridges, including the Brooklyn Bridge in New York City, with the intent of bringing them down. Given KSM's training as an engineer and his past record of inventing simple ways to bring down office towers, I was not ready to dismiss his desires as impossible or even improbable.

In tribunal filings at Guantanamo Bay, the U.S. military reported that KSM had admitted playing a role in at least thirty-one terror plots around the world. Some, like the 9/11 attacks, had tragically succeeded. Others, like the December 2001 "shoe bomber" attack, had been narrowly averted. And still others, such as plans to attack the tallest building in Los Angeles, the Sears Tower in Chicago, and the Plaza Bank building in Seattle, had been in the works as a possible second wave following the September 11 atrocity and fortunately never took place. The plots were by no means limited to the U.S. KSM confirmed plans to attack London's Heathrow Airport and Canary Wharf, NATO's European headquarters in Belgium, and U.S. embassies and consulates in a variety of locations.

I cannot stress strongly enough that we did not take any of these claims at face value. The planned attacks on Heathrow and Canary Wharf, for example, were things we first heard about from Ramzi bin al-Shibh when the Pakistanis captured him on September 11, 2002. A little over six months later KSM, completely independently, verified what we had been told and provided deep detail about what could have been a devastating attack.

Here is a little-known and little-credited example of how, after he became compliant, KSM provided information that led to the unraveling of some other very dangerous plots.

In 2003 KSM told us that at some point in the late 1990s he had sent an al-Qa'ida operative who used the nom de guerre Issa al-Britani to Kuala Lumpur, Malaysia, to "learn about jihad" in Southeast Asia from Hambali. KSM said that a couple of years later, bin Ladin sent al-Britani to the United States to scout out potential economic and what he deemed "Jewish" targets in and around New York City. We took the information very seriously but at the time did not have enough actionable information to immediately track down al-Britani. He certainly became an important target for us.

We passed on KSM's information, not only to our British counterparts (based on the "al-Britani" nickname) but also to the 9/11 Commission. They included part of his story in their final report, which was published on July 22, 2004. So keep in mind, the commission is repeating reports about terrorists not yet in custody. These reports were furnished to us by KSM after he had been subjected to EITs.

Just three days after the 9/11 Commission report was released, the Pakistanis, working with the CIA, captured two terrorists. One was someone by the name of Ahmed Gailani, who was wanted in connection with the 1998 East African Embassy bombings. In addition to the individuals, we picked up one of their computers, which had on it highly detailed casing reports on economic institutions in New York and Washington, and these reports were signed "Issa al-Britani," just as KSM had told us.

We passed on additional information that was picked up in Pakistan to the British and on August 3, 2004, they were able to arrest a British subject by the name of Dhiren Barot. It turned out Barot had a handful of aka's, including Abu Musa al-Hindi, Abu Issa al-Hindi, and Issa al-Britani.

An Indian-born Muslim convert, Barot had moved to Britain as a small child. As a young man he had worked for an airline in London. During their investigation British police learned that Barot had traveled to Pakistan to undergo training at al-Qa'ida-related camps.

He was the author of a thirty-nine-page memo instructing fellow al-Qa'ida supporters on how to construct devastating explosives using everyday materials that could be obtained in hardware stores or pharmacies.

Just as KSM had told us, Barot had traveled to the U.S. in 2000 and had done extensive surveillance of places like the Prudential Building in New Jersey, the New York Stock Exchange and Citigroup in New York, and the International Monetary Fund headquarters in Washington. British authorities were able to seize more than fifty compact discs with the targeting data he had assembled. CIA officers who reviewed the material were stunned at the sophistication and completeness of the casing he had conducted. It was so professionally done that one officer told me it looked as if it had been conducted by a highly skilled Western intelligence operative.

Peter Clarke, deputy assistant commissioner of the Metropolitan Police Counterterrorism Command, was quoted in the *Guardian* newspaper as saying: "By his own admission Barot wanted to commit mass murder on both sides of the Atlantic. He was the leader of the plot. If he had succeeded, hundreds if not thousands could have died."

In addition to the information about plots against financial institutions, Barot's holdings included information about planning to use limousines packed with explosives in attacks in the U.K. and the U.S. He had studied the work of the Oklahoma

City bombers and, given the chance, might have emulated that devastating attack. The materials found with Barot also showed that he had a desire to blow up a London Tube train while it passed under the Thames River. His hope was to cause a rupture to the train tunnel, killing passengers both from the explosion and from drowning. Some observers thought that his plans were fanciful. Eleven months after Barot was captured, on July 7, 2005, al-Qa'ida did strike the London transit system, killing fifty-two people and injuring more than seven hundred. Barot was convicted of conspiracy to commit murder and was sentenced to life imprisonment in 2006. His sentence was later reduced by British courts to thirty years.

Each time we uncovered evidence of a viable al-Qa'ida plot, even if we were confident we had preempted it, it gave us cause for concern. One of the hallmarks of al-Qa'ida is that they always return to failed plots and try, try again.

The most obvious example, of course, was the World Trade Center, which was attacked in 1993 and again in 2001. But there were others. Al-Qa'ida tried to blow up a U.S. Navy guided-missile destroyer, USS *The Sullivans,* in Aden in January 2000. That attempt went awry but they were back in October of that same year with a tragically successful attack on the USS *Cole.* So when we learned of potentially disrupted plans to attack buildings in Los Angeles or Chicago, or of a desire to use dirty bombs in New York or Washington, or plans to bring down suspension bridges crossing the Hudson or East rivers, we never had the luxury of thinking, "Well, that threat is over."

Success after success was being racked up. Often the news of some major al-Qa'ida operative's being arrested or killed would leak or be announced only hours after the event itself. Quite a few of the people taken down were described as the "number-three" person in al-Qa'ida. This resulted in a good deal of skepticism on the part of outside observers. "How many 'number threes' do these guys have?" we'd be asked. In truth, it is often difficult to ascribe an exact pecking order position to people within groups like al-Qa'ida, but in fact we did have enormous success in taking out senior operational leaders.

I understood the frustration expressed by some who wanted to know: "Why are you always getting number three when we'd much rather see you get number one (UBL) and number two (Ayman al-Zawahiri)?" There was a reason, however, why the longevity of number threes was so low. Guys like bin Ladin and Zawahiri were the highest-ranking executives in the world-wide organization known as al-Qa'ida. They set broad strategy but could afford to lie low. By definition, number threes, the COOs of the organization, had to be out there *operating*. They had to be moving around, using cell phones and radios, main-taining contact with other members and actively trying to fo-ment more plots. As they raised their heads above the foxholes, we picked them off one by one.

I created quite a controversy in May 2011 when, in rare public comments, I told a *Time* magazine correspondent that information that came from KSM and another senior al-Qa'ida detainee, Abu Faraj al-Libi, eventually led to the location of bin Ladin's compound and the operation that resulted in UBL's death. My comment (to use former vice president Cheney's phrase) caused heads to explode around Washington. People who had a stake in denigrating the impact and effectiveness of the EITs rushed out to counter my statement.

Time quoted National Security Council spokesman Tommy Vietor as saying: "There is no way that information obtained by [EITs] was the decisive intelligence that led us directly to bin Ladin. It took years of collection and analysis from many different sources to develop the case that enabled us to identify this compound and reach a judgment that bin Ladin was likely to be living there."

With all due respect, Mr. Vietor doesn't understand how the EIT program worked. I never said that the EITs were the immediate cause, or that they instantly led us to UBL. But without the EITs we might never have started on the long march that eventually allowed CIA analysts to come to the conclusion that UBL was probably holed up in Abbottabad. Here is how that journey began.

An al-Qa'ida operative was captured in 2004. He was quickly turned over to the CIA. He had computer discs with him that showed that he was relaying information between al-Qa'ida and Abu Musab Zarqawi, AQ's terrorist leader in Iraq who was responsible for a large number of bombings, beheadings, and other attacks. Zarqawi worked hard to provoke sectarian violence between Iraqi Shia and Sunni communities, with the goal of spreading general chaos in that war-ravaged country. So having this operative in our custody was of great interest.

We moved him to a black site and began the effort to find out what other information he might have that we could exploit. Initially, he played the role of a tough mujahideen and refused to cooperate. We then received permission to use some (but not all) of the EIT procedures on him. Before long he became compliant and started to provide some excellent information. As with all the al-Qa'ida operatives, we asked him about the organization's leadership and how they were continuing to function. He told us that bin Ladin conducted business by using a trusted courier with whom he was in contact only sporadically. He said that the Sheikh (as bin Ladin was referred to by his subordinates) stayed completely away from telephones, radios, or the internet in an effort to frustrate American attempts to find him. And frustrated we were.

We pressed him on who this courier was and he said all he knew was a pseudonym: "Abu Ahmed al-Kuwaiti." This was a critical bit of information about the identity of the man who would eventually lead us to bin Ladin.

The news was remarkable for a number of reasons. He provided a very promising lead that might provide a path to UBL but he also gave us an insight into the way al-Qa'ida was being run. You can't effectively run any organization, be it a business or a terrorist group, when the senior management communicates with subordinates only several times a year. We gained the impression that UBL was functioning more like a chairman of the board than a CEO.

Armed with the information from this detainee, as we always did, we tried to verify it by asking other senior detainees about what we had just learned. It is important to keep in mind that the most knowledgeable and hardened AQ leaders never told us everything they knew. They tried to shield their most important secrets, but nevertheless, once they were compliant, started (sometimes inadvertently) to fill in the blanks. One of our debriefers had asked a senior detainee who had recently become compliant, "What is your biggest fear?" Without hesitation he answered, "I fear that I might accidentally tell you something that leads you to the Sheikh."

So Agency officers went to KSM and asked him, "What can you tell us about Abu Ahmed al-Kuwaiti?" KSM's eyes grew wide and he backed up into his cell. He said no words but spoke volumes with his actions. We later asked Abu Faraj al-Libi, one of those famous short-term al-Qa'ida "number threes," who was captured in May 2005, about the courier. Al-Libi admitted that a courier like the one we described was the person who had informed him that he had been elevated to the status of AQ's operational leader. That kind of information and assignment isn't entrusted to a run-of-the-mill runner. We figured a courier empowered to deliver the news that someone had been anointed "number three" had to be well wired with "number one." Al-Libi vehemently denied, however, that he had ever met a courier named al-Kuwaiti. His denial was so vociferous that it was obvious to us that he was trying to hide something very important.

Now critics will tell you: "See, EITs didn't work. Otherwise KSM and Abu Faraj al-Libi would have given the CIA the true name of the courier when you asked them about it." But such critics fail to understand how the program worked. Without EITs, AQ operatives would have had little incentive to tell us anything. With them, they told us much, but not everything we wanted to know. We didn't twist their arms (literally or figuratively) every time we had a new question. But we watched them and learned much. Sometimes what they didn't say, and the accompanying body language, gave us critical clues.

By now we were pretty convinced that this mysterious courier by the name of Abu Ahmed al-Kuwaiti could be the key to unlock the mystery we most wanted to solve: Where is bin Ladin?

From that point on, finding Abu Ahmed al-Kuwaiti became one of our top intelligence-collection priorities. About two years later we learned the true name of the man we sought. That was progress, but it wasn't enough. Now the CIA had to find him.

One of my biggest regrets is that we were not able to find this man while I was at the Agency. The courier exercised excellent tradecraft, maintaining a low profile and generally avoiding using methods of communication that might trip him up. Then, sometime after I left the CIA, he made a mistake. He slipped and did something that allowed U.S. intelligence to find him. From there, using great patience and skill, CIA officers eventually were able to trace him to the compound in Abbottabad and assemble the intelligence case that led to the successful raid on May 2, 2011. It all started with information a detainee provided after receiving EITs bolstered by information that KSM and Abu Faraj al-Libi (who both became compliant after receiving EITs) gave us, whether they meant to or not.

President Obama and his national security team deserve great credit for following the trail to its conclusion and making the gutsy decision to send in the U.S. special operations forces team that performed so magnificently. In the immediate aftermath, some of the president's senior staff "committed truth"— they confirmed the role the EITs played in bringing UBL to his much-deserved demise. Then–CIA director Leon Panetta told NBC's Brian Williams, "We had multiple series of sources that provided information with regards to this situation . . . clearly some of it came from detainees [and] they used these enhanced interrogation techniques against some of those detainees." Williams followed up by asking Panetta if waterboarding was part of the "enhanced interrogation techniques" that he had just mentioned and Panetta said: "That's correct."

As difficult as conducting interrogation and debriefings at secret locations might be, none of it would have been possible without the CIA's ability to quickly, safely, and quietly move detainees around the world. This capability has widely and inaccurately been dubbed "torture flights" by some in the chattering class. They were nothing of the sort.

While there is much that I still cannot reveal about the process, I am free to lift the veil a bit on some of it. The CIA first got involved in making significant international moves of prisoners not after 9/11 but in the early 1990s during the Clinton administration. More than seventy prisoners had been clandestinely moved in the seven years leading up to September 11.

Moving detainees around clandestinely is an extraordinarily difficult thing to do. The officers in the Agency's branch in charge of renditions had become very adept at it. Over the years, the CIA has had the use of a small fleet of special aircraft.

Almost invariably, missions would arise with little or no notice and it would be necessary to get an aircraft quickly and quietly to some remote location and just as quickly and quietly spirit a high-value passenger off to another location. The planning of such missions was very precise. Renditions branch officers prided themselves on having an aircraft on the ground at the ultimate destination at whatever time was stated in the operational plan. Sometimes we would be unable to tell the pilots where they were going until they were in the air. Even then, at times the ultimate destination changed while they were en route.

On the ground at a stop, aircraft wait their turn for a refueling truck. Our officers, when in a rush (which was generally the case), would find the ground support personnel and start peeling off hundred-dollar bills to ensure our place at the head of the refueling queue.

The team we had working on transportation was nothing if not resourceful. I remember one instance in which one of our aircraft landed in a remote spot. While it was on the ground, a local airport worker lost control of a forklift and punched a hole in the wing of our bird. The crew sent a digital picture of the damage back to the States along with their plan, which was to cover the puncture with duct tape. They did, and completed the mission. A week or so later the aircraft made it home to the U.S., where the damage was repaired.

On another occasion we had two aircraft trying to get to a very remote location. There were mountains surrounding the airfield. The weather was awful, with visibility at about 250 feet. To make matters worse, the field had no navigation aids, no tower, and no lights. No one on either airplane had been to the location before. After several abortive attempts to land, they were able to reach one of our contacts on the ground. That person drove his jeep onto the runway and flashed his headlights, providing enough of a beacon for the first airplane to land.

As conditions worsened, the airplane on the ground positioned itself on the end of the runway with its right wing on the centerline. Blinking its nose light, it provided just enough guidance for the second plane to find the airstrip through the mist and fog and touch down at the opposite end of the runway. As the second arrival rolled toward them, the crew of the first plane found themselves praying that the brakes on the other airplane worked well. They did.

There are lots of stories floating around about how detainees were treated on these flights. The stories almost always suggest that our "guests" were abused and mistreated from the moment they boarded the aircraft. Like so much that has been written about our efforts, this, too, is wrong.

The onboard team would mark down any bumps, bruises, bandages, scars, or anomalies that the detainee might have. They wanted to be able to demonstrate when they got to their ultimate destination that the passenger was in the same condition in which he boarded.

When moving hardened terrorists on long, international flights, you don't want to have to deal with taking passengers to use the tiny onboard airplane lavatory. So the detainees were given sedatives, and they slept through much of the lengthy journey. Throughout the flight, Agency personnel checked their vital signs and made sure they were properly hydrated.

Most often there were only one or two detainees on a flight. There were times, however, such as when we had to close down one black site and open another, that as many as fourteen detainees were moved on a single flight. The logistics for such a complex operation were demanding.

The arrangements at the black sites were similarly precise. We took great pains to construct facilities that would safely and securely contain the detainees while maximizing our ability to gather intelligence from them. Since we had never been in the detention business, Agency officers visited the U.S. Bureau of Prisons to learn about how to create the most effective holding facility.

Our sites were designed to create a complete loss of orientation on the part of the detainees. They were in a completely sterile environment with no distractions. They had no idea where they were or what was going on outside their cell, let alone elsewhere in the world. There was one thing we did that ran against the concept of disorientation. Each holding cell had an arrow painted on the floor pointed toward Mecca for prayers. Our officers charged with constructing the holding facilities took compasses into each cell to make sure they accurately indicated the direction toward the Ka'aba, the holiest place in Islam.

Occasionally, attempts to spruce up the detainees' living quarters were rebuffed, however. For example, at one point, after they had become compliant, Agency officers hung some posters in the detainees' cells. Ramzi bin al-Shibh objected, however, because the poster in his cell had a picture of a bird on it. "Only Allah can make images of birds!" he said, and he demanded the poster be removed. It was.

The sense of isolation alone was sufficient to motivate many of the detainees to begin cooperation. Whether they cooperated or not, we took exceptionally good care of them. The detainees had access to outstanding medical, dental, and even vision care. When one of the detainees developed an infected toe, we flew in a specialist to deal with it. The medical care they received far exceeded that which was available to their captors.

The food the detainees received was *halal*—prepared in ways acceptable to Islam. The food our officers ate was often less scrupulously crafted. At one site Agency officers termed the typical meal "chork"—because they were uncertain whether it was chicken or pork.

In the early days of their detention, some of the al-Qa'ida operatives were placed on reduced-calorie diets, relying heavily on liquid Ensure, which, true to its name, ensured that the detainees received sufficient vitamins and nutrients. Some of our guests grew quite fond of the drink. Khalid Sheikh Mohammed, in particular, was a huge fan of chocolate Ensure. When one of our senior officers who was with KSM during his first few weeks of detention saw him again about a year later, KSM patted his vastly reduced waistline and proclaimed: "See, the CIA diet works! I've been trying to lose weight for years, but you guys know the secret." KSM became so weight conscious that he maintained his own chart in his cell happily tracking his ever-diminishing girth.

After the detainees became cooperative, Agency officers worked hard to keep them relatively happy. The detainees were asked for a list of reading material they would like to have, and CIA officers would go out and purchase the books and operate a lending library for all their "guests."

Within hours of our capture of Abu Zubaydah, the world knew that he was in custody somewhere. The word of the takedown of other senior AQ leaders quickly became public knowledge as well. At first the media seemed to accept that these terrorists were being held somewhere without much question. There were lots of leaks (authorized and not) about some of the information we were gaining from our debriefings.

After a while, the media started an all-out effort to uncover and expose where the detainees were being held. It was not an easy thing for them to find out. We deliberately kept the circle of people who knew where the black sites were to a very small number. We didn't tell the FBI. We told only the highest levels of the State Department. Many people, even those within the

Agency with the highest security clearances, were not clued in. As far as I know, the location of the black sites was not even shared with the president. It is not that senior White House officials weren't trusted, but rather that they simply did not have a "need to know."

After a while, media accounts speculating about the location of the black sites, and the conditions under which the detainees were being held, started to emerge. Many of these accounts were wrong. But eventually some started getting closer to the truth. At one point when one news organization was about to report on the location of the site where Abu Zubaydah and others were being held, I made the decision to quickly close that site and send our detainees to another location thousands of miles away.

Several times during my tenure we felt obliged to close one well-functioning facility and move to another because we were unable to maintain the secrecy of the site. It became so routine that we started causing additional black sites to be constructed in anticipation of the current ones being exposed.

I remember that we had spent millions of dollars building a new facility on another continent thousands of miles away. The chief of that country's intelligence service urgently asked to come see me. He appeared to be tremendously embarrassed when I met with him. He nervously confessed that the heat was just too much from journalists (mostly American) who were sniffing around trying to find where we might be holding the worst terrorists on the planet. "Mr. Rodriguez," he said to me, "my country simply cannot take the risk of helping yours in this way." I told him I understood, and regretted that we had put them in an awkward position. It made no sense to express anger or frustration with him, and besides, I hoped there would be other, less-onerous ways for him and his country to help us in the future.

In the fall of 2005, *Washington Post* reporter Dana Priest was working on a story that eventually was called "CIA Holds Terror Suspects in Secret Prisons." Hearing that such a story was about to be published, the CIA director, Porter Goss, asked me to meet with her, off-the-record, to see if I could convince her that such a story would harm U.S. national security, put some of our allies around the world in a very difficult position, and potentially disrupt a program that was providing intelligence that was producing real results and helping keep the country safe.

I was still undercover at the time, and my full name was not publicly known (although some media had reported that the head of CIA's operations was a person who could be described only as "Jose"). I was quite happy to have had almost no dealings with American journalists in my decades of Agency service. From what I knew about the media's passion for revealing anything secret, I had little hope of convincing Priest to keep the black sites in the dark. But the stakes were high, so I agreed to give it a shot.

Priest was escorted to my office and presented me with an unsolicited autographed copy of a book she had written the previous year about the U.S. military. That failed to soften my stance on the lack of wisdom of her proceeding with her article as planned. She laid out a rough outline of what she planned to write. While she had some facts wrong, she had others uncomfortably right. I made my case for why such an article—right or wrong—would be damaging. I could see I was not winning her over. In the end, the *Post* did agree to fuzz up some information about the location of supposed sites, but the overall impact of the article and others that followed and expanded on it was most unhelpful.

One final story on the black site shuffle. When we grew concerned that the identity of the first location where Abu

Zubaydah was interrogated was about to leak, I issued an order that the facility be closed in ninety-six hours and the detainees be moved to a new site. The Agency officers on scene quickly began packing up the material they needed to take with them to the next location and destroying anything else so as to leave no reminders of what had taken place there. Agency officers serving in hot spots around the world are quite accustomed to minimizing their footprint in case they have to "bug out" on short notice. In this case, the base chief sought guidance on a number of things, including a pile of ninety-two videotapes that were stacked in a jumble on a bookcase in her office. The tapes had been made during the early days of AZ's interrogation. Some midlevel person in CTC, whose name I do not know, correctly believing that we weren't getting any useful intelligence from the tapes, recommended that they be thrown onto a bonfire that was being lit nearby. The tapes were scooped up and about to be turned into useless slag when a follow-up cable from headquarters came in saying: "Hold up on the tapes. We think they should be retained for a little while longer." Had that message been delayed by even a few minutes, my life in the years following would have been considerably easier.

On September 17, 2001, President Bush gave the CIA extraordinary authority in pursuing the terrorist threat. Presidential authorizations are mechanisms by which the Agency carries out its covert clandestine activities. Despite the popular misconception, we didn't freelance or just make things up as we went along. The parameters of significant actions are clearly laid out and the Agency is told what it can and cannot do, when and where it can do it, and what tools are at its disposal. These authorities are briefed to the leadership of the House and Senate intelligence committees and to the appropriations committees to facilitate oversight as well.

The September 17 authorities were sweeping in scope. We were authorized to go after al-Qa'ida leaders around the world and bring them down so that they could not orchestrate another terrorist attack like the devastating one that had happened less than a week before. While the identity and general location of the principal targets were fairly well known (Usama bin Ladin and his top aides were generally thought to be in Afghanistan and Pakistan), it was clear that this was truly a "global" war on terror. Al-Qa'ida had contacts and operatives in a score of countries. Going after them in a war zone was fairly straightforward. But what of those who might be hiding in plain sight elsewhere? Obviously, where local governments were willing and able to assist, these individuals became targets of law enforcement that would seek to detain, interrogate, and arrest them. In some cases, we found it necessary and useful to "assist" terrorists to get from where they were to somewhere else where their interrogation could be ensured. This was the "rendition" program I discussed earlier. The term "extraordinary rendition" was an invention of the press.

It occurred to me, however, that potentially there was another category of person—a known bad actor of the worst sort who was living not in a war zone but somewhere from which we could not remove him via such proceedings as extradition or by rendition. It seemed to me that for a superpower like the United States, the president should have at his disposal the capability of removing that person permanently in order to protect U.S. interests.

There was already plenty of authority, if we could find a terrorist in a war zone, for the president to order B-52s to carpet-bomb his location—or fire scores of cruise missiles into the area where he was believed to be hiding. Should we not, we asked ourselves, have the capability to much more surgically remove a threat when other means, such as arrest, are not available? The military had the capability, using special operations forces units such as Navy SEALS, to parachute into a situation and take strong military action, as they demonstrated nearly a decade later when they killed Usama bin Ladin. Most major police forces have SWAT teams with snipers who can be used in criminal standoffs. But, despite the popularity of Jason Bourne movies or Mitch Rapp novels, there was no such capability for the president to order the *clandestine* elimination of an existential threat to the United States outside a foreign war zone.

I fully understood that this would be highly controversial and a capability that would be used under the most rare and dire circumstances, if at all. But I thought that if the circumstances ever arose in which the country needed such know-how, it would be too late to try to develop the necessary skills or to establish the legal basis for allowing us to use them.

I believe there should be a thoughtful debate about what is necessary and moral for a country to survive. It had been the policy of the U.S. government since the Clinton administration, fully approved by Congress, to support regime change in Iraq. If Saddam could have been removed with a single bullet, might that not have been preferable to a war that killed hundreds of thousands of Iraqis, cost thousands of American lives, created tens of thousands of amputees, and saddled U.S. taxpayers with estimated direct costs of nearly $1 trillion? More recently, more than $1 billion was expended by the United States and hundreds of millions more by our NATO allies to try to remove Libya's Muammar Qadhafi from power. Thousands of people were killed in the operation; many were noncombatants. Officials danced around trying to explain how airstrikes on Qadhafi's residences and offices were not designed to kill him. Is it less moral to have a leader like Qadhafi succumb to what some euphemistically referred to as "the ultimate brush pass," or to bomb his headquarters, hoping he somehow meets his demise, along with the hundreds or perhaps thousands of others who surely will be collateral damage?

The answers to these questions are not easy. I recognize that there is an argument that taking out political leaders or terrorists outside a war zone may, in the mind of some, legitimize attacks on Western leaders. The counterargument, of course, is that our leaders are already targeted. I am not arguing for broad-based or promiscuous use of operations, but giving up the option without understanding what is at stake strikes me as exceedingly unwise.

Chapter 6

REGIME CHANGE

As 2003 rolled into 2004, those of us in CTC continued to rack up successes. Building on the information we were obtaining from senior detainees in our custody, we were able to deliver some serious blows to al-Qa'ida. But the CIA itself was taking some hits as well.

Following the 2003 invasion of Iraq, the Agency came under heavy criticism when the weapons of mass destruction (WMD) that virtually everyone believed Saddam had, and that some relied on to justify the war, failed to turn up. My personal involvement in the run-up to and immediate aftermath of what the Pentagon dubbed "Operation Iraqi Freedom" was slight. My entire focus was on terrorism. There were some in the administration, particularly on the staff of Vice President Cheney, who were hell-bent on connecting Saddam and his regime to al-Qa'ida. They repeatedly asked our analysts to dig through the data looking for threads that might connect the two. We found precious little. Although Saddam had supported other terrorist operations in the past, connections between Iraq and AQ were remarkably thin. I could have given you a list of a half-dozen countries that had more substantial ties to bin Ladin's organization than did Iraq.

Whether Iraq had connections to 9/11 was a legitimate question, and had we found any, the case for going to war with Baghdad would have been easy to make. But when we disappointed those who were seeking those connections, they moved on to rely on other things, such as WMD.

The Agency was also taking heat from the 9/11 Commission and from other investigations trying to get to the bottom of the September 11 attacks. It is a natural human instinct to try to learn from disastrous events like that and sadly, it is natural for some people to look for others to blame. The relatively small group of officers within CTC who had been obsessed with Usama bin Ladin, years before almost anyone else in our government even knew his name, came under particularly close scrutiny. With the clarity of 20/20 hindsight, it was easy for critics who knew how events had unfolded to cherry-pick a few nuggets of information from the mountains of data that these officers were dealing with before 9/11 and years later say, "How could you have missed this?"

One of my challenges was to keep these fine officers, unquestionably the world's leading experts on al-Qa'ida, focused on the continuing struggle to stop the next attack and to get UBL while they were at the same time being grilled by commission staffers, IG office investigators, and others who had an outcome in mind and were simply working backward to fill in the blanks to justify their conclusions.

If the importance of our mission had not been so great, and so obvious, it would have been impossible to get any human being to focus on the enemy abroad while being sniped at by others at home. But having lived through the horror of 9/11, these officers, many of them women, as it turned out, knew better than anyone the stakes at hand.

The 9/11 Commission report did get some things right. Among them was the statement that "before 9/11, no agency did more to attack al-Qa'ida than the CIA." The commission's final report was widely praised in the media for how fully it told the story of how al-Qa'ida created and carried out the 9/11 plot. Two chapters of their report (Chapter 5, "Al Qaeda Aims at the American Homeland," and Chapter 7, "The Attack Looms") were heavily based on information gleaned by the CIA's interrogation program. Those who claim nothing useful came out of the Agency's debriefing of senior AQ operatives are almost always mute on this point.

In early June, George Tenet announced that he would be stepping down a month later. He had held the job for seven years and was the second-longest-serving DCI in Agency history. Many of my junior officers had known no other DCI. George was tired. Tired of the grind and even more worn down by the beating he was taking from politicians, pundits, and armchair "terrorism experts." I was sad to see him depart but understood why he felt it was time for him to go.

Truth be told, I was very tired myself and was looking forward to a day not too far away when I too could lay my burden down. Some treat it as a joke when government officials announce their departure and say they want to spend more time with their family. But in high-pressure jobs, despite the best efforts to find some balance, families are short-changed too often. In my case, our two boys were reaching college age, and the thought of finding a job with smaller demands on my time and larger paychecks was a considerable attraction.

Early in 2004, I was asked to consult with the organizers of that summer's Olympic Games in Athens. That international gathering was a prime potential target for terrorists, and we were all relieved when, amid heavy security precautions, no terrorist incidents took place. The experience of advising the government of Greece convinced me that I might have a productive and lucrative second career ahead as a consultant. But while there were things pulling me toward the door, there was one factor that kept me in place: the sense of unfinished business. Having been in CTC since the hours immediately after 9/11, I wanted to be part of the team that would bring al-Qa'ida's leaders to justice.

George Tenet had been CTC's biggest supporter. He fought to get us the tools we needed and the authorization to use them. He was a frequent visitor to CTC windowless spaces far below his airy seventh-floor office. He has a special gift of leadership, which allowed him to constantly ride us for more productive performance while always seeming to be our champion and never a nag. I will forever be grateful to him for having the confidence to make an unlikely candidate like me chief of CTC.

John McLaughlin, George's deputy, is probably as unlike Tenet as it is possible to be in terms of personality. Yet the two of them made a superb team. While Tenet is garrulous and voluble, McLaughlin is soft-spoken and professorial. They complemented each other better than any other one-two team at CIA I had ever witnessed.

So we were delighted to see McLaughlin placed in charge as acting director when Tenet stepped down. In the post-9/11 environment there has never been a quiet time at the CIA, and it certainly wasn't calm during the period when McLaughlin was in charge. His tenure at the top coincided with one of the periods when the Department of Justice started to moonwalk away from us on the authorities they had previously provided regarding interrogation. As it happened, we had just captured a fairly senior al-Qa'ida operative when DOJ started to waver on the legality of the program. John courageously said that we would shut it down to protect our officers if we didn't have clear guidance from our political masters. That stance did not go down well with senior officials at the White House. But John said he was not going to have our officers undertake any actions knowing that their government might later claim they were illegal. Eventually the DOJ came through with the renewed authorities and the interrogation and debriefing resumed.

The summer of 2004 was a difficult time. The country was in the middle of a presidential campaign, and the conduct of intelligence had become a political football. The comparative unity Americans had achieved in the days following 9/11 was a thing of the past. Many of our elected leaders were positioning themselves and posturing to make political hay out of the trau-'matic experience of the past couple of years.

The 9/11 Commission report, released on July 22, 2004, was harshly critical of the structure and performance of the American intelligence community and, among other things, recommended the creation of a "national intelligence director" to supervise the work of the sixteen agencies that made up the intelligence community (IC).

We had already undergone some wrenching reorganization, which seems to be a bureaucracy's way of giving the impression (often false) of progress. In 2003, with little prior discussion or study, the Bush administration announced the creation of the Terrorist Threat Integration Center (TTIC), which was designed to facilitate the sharing of terrorist information (by brute force if necessary) across the many elements of the IC that collected and analyzed that information.

The TTIC later evolved into the National Counter Terrorist Center (NCTC), which should not be confused with the CIA's CTC. The creation of such an organization was probably a good thing, but the way it was accomplished was not. In order to help man the new organization, a decision was made to rip most, if not all, of the top CT analysts out of CTC. I was strongly against such a move. Why take the one part of the U.S. government's counterterrorist structure that was working best and weaken it to create some new, untried entity? In our briefings to the 9/11 Commission our warning to them was that whatever changes were subsequently implemented, the most important thing was to do no harm. I lost that argument regarding TTIC, and a healthy chunk of CTC's best analysts were shipped to the new organization, which was created under the leadership of John Brennan, who at the time was the CIA's deputy executive director. Now, having painfully survived that reorganization, there was talk about a larger restructuring of the IC. I couldn't afford to let my people be distracted by all the talk of rewiring the Rube Goldberg–like structure of the intelligence community. We had a war to fight.

On August 2, President Bush invited Acting-DCI John McLaughlin, Secretary of State Powell, and others to the White House, where (much to the surprise of many present) he announced that his administration was backing the creation of a director of national intelligence (DNI). While the idea of such an organization had been kicked around for many years, this announcement had the air about it of something done for political expediency. Senator John Kerry, the Democratic nominee for president, had endorsed the 9/11 Commission's recommendations in their entirety and the administration appeared to be rushing to get to the head of the parade. Some inside the intelligence community, such as John McLaughlin, had previously warned that the DNI structure was unnecessary. Others worried that it would be unwieldy, although White House and NSC staffers assured them that the DNI staff would be supervisory, in charge of coordinating and empowering the existing intelligence community. It would be small and nimble, they said, numbering seven hundred people or fewer. (According to press accounts, within five years the staff had grown to over two thousand, more than the total of people in CTC during my tenure.)

Shortly after announcing his plan to create the DNI, President Bush nominated Congressman Porter Goss, the chairman of the House Permanent Select Committee on Intelligence (HPSCI), to become the last DCI. The plan was that once the DNI position was established, Goss would lead the CIA but someone else would come in to take the overarching DNI slot.

If the president wanted to bring in new leadership for the

CIA, Goss was an obvious choice. He had been a CIA case officer during the 1960s. After leaving the Agency and becoming successful in business, Goss got into politics, eventually being elected to Congress representing the Fourteenth Congressional District in southwest Florida.

Goss had been chair of the oversight committee that closely monitored the CIA for about seven years. Few Americans outside the Agency knew as much about its inner workings as did he.

My interaction with Goss when he was chairman of HPSCI was always good. In hearings and briefings he always asked tough, penetrating questions but did so in a respectful fashion, making clear that he was looking for answers, not opportunities to score political points. So I was fairly optimistic that Goss would only build on the positive experience we in CTC had under the leadership of George Tenet and John McLaughlin.

What I didn't count on was that Goss would bring in with him a handful of senior aides, mostly former congressional staffers, who had an agenda of their own. Some of these people had had brief assignments at the CIA in the past, but many knew us only from their perspective as congressional staffers. Many of the people around Goss came in with a collective chip on their shoulders, many pledging openly to fix what they perceived to be the badly broken organization that was the CIA. They had the arrogance of armchair quarterbacks who had never played the game but were ready to tell battle-scarred veterans that they were all screwed up. Just months before he was tapped to lead the CIA, Goss's staff had drafted a signing statement to accompany the FY 2005 Intelligence Authorization Bill, which flatly stated that things were so bad at the CIA that we were on the verge of being incapable of "the slightest bit of success." To the people who had routed al-Qa'ida from Afghanistan, captured Abu Zubaydah and KSM, brought down the

A. Q. Khan network (which proliferated nuclear technology to rogue nations), and convinced Libya to turn over its WMD without firing a shot, the claim was bitterly received.

In addition to thinking we were incompetent, many on Goss's team, who were collectively awarded the derisive nickname of "the Gosslings," also thought the CIA was actively working to undermine the reelection chances of President Bush. They cited leaks to the press of gloomy intelligence estimates about progress in Iraq or anonymous comments in the media attributed to current and former intelligence officials to bolster their case. My experience was that CIA was not a very political place at all. People there knew a lot about the governments of foreign nations but weren't particularly focused on the politics of their own.

Goss's leadership style, of not getting down in the weeds and letting your people have wide-ranging flexibility, works well when you have good people. Although there were a few exceptions, unfortunately, many of the men Goss brought into the CIA with him let him down badly and quickly. It was a shame. I always thought that Goss gave his heart and soul to the Agency and cared about its mission and people deeply. He deserved much better.

Most of the jobs to be filled by the team Goss brought in with him were important but publicly invisible positions within the Agency. One exception was the executive director's job, which, in Agency hierarchy, was considered the third-ranking position at the CIA. The "ExDir," as the holder of the position was known, was the person in charge of day-to-day operations of the Agency. He was someone who kept the trains running on time and served as sort of the COO of the CIA. In that role this person was responsible for many of the management functions, including enforcing rules and regulations and applying discipline to those Agency officers who transgressed.

Goss elected to replace Buzzy Krongard, the hyperefficient, tough-as-nails former business executive whom Tenet had installed in the position, with Michael Kostiw. Kostiw had worked as a CIA case officer for about ten years in the 1970s, had later worked on Capitol Hill, and had been a vice president for ChevronTexaco.

As is the case in all appointments, Agency security officials review the files of nominees to make sure there are no reasons why that person might not be suitable for a particular job. There were some things of concern in Kostiw's past, and Goss's incoming chief of staff (one of the people brought in from the Hill), Pat Murray, was so informed. Murray reportedly was not troubled by the information and on September 30, six days after Goss was sworn in, an announcement went out to the Agency workforce about Goss's plan to install various people in new slots starting the next week. The announcement included Murray's own appointment and those of Goss's personal secretary and two other senior officials, plus Kostiw's assignment as ExDir. Much of the same information was reported in the *Washington Post* the following day.

The next afternoon, Friday, October 2, Agency officials sent out a copy of the announcement in an email to thousands of retired CIA officers around the country who routinely receive administrative notes from their old employer.

The very next day, there was a story in the *Washington Post* by longtime intelligence writer Walter Pincus, reporting that Kostiw had resigned from the Agency in 1981 following allegations that he had been caught shoplifting. Subsequent press stories said that the item in question was a pound of bacon from a local Safeway store.

The palace guard around Goss were furious. They were mad not about having mistakenly put someone in charge of good order and discipline at the CIA who had left the Agency under an ethical cloud but because someone had shared the rumors of Kostiw's past with the media. They were convinced this was another example of currently serving Agency officers defying their will.

Goss's team put up a brief but vigorous fight for their man, but after a couple of days of bad press it was clear that it was a losing battle. On October 4 the Agency released a statement from Kostiw saying: "As a result of recent press articles and attendant speculation, I have decided that I cannot accept an appointment as CIA's Executive Director." Instead, he took a much lower-profile position as a senior advisor to Goss. Ironically, of all the people Goss brought with him to CIA, Kostiw turned out to be one of the most competent, hardworking, humble, and well liked. It is a shame that circumstances prevented him from serving in the ExDir role. I personally enjoyed a very good relationship with Mike and respected his counsel. If the other men Goss brought in had been more like him, Goss's stay at the CIA would have been longer and happier.

You might wonder why I am relating this decades-old story of purloined bacon. It clearly has nothing to do with counterterrorism. But oddly, the incident set off a chain reaction of events that had a profound impact on the rest of my career.

Once Kostiw withdrew, the outsiders Goss had brought in gathered to find another candidate to be ExDir. Once again they outsmarted themselves. Somehow they came up with the name of Kyle "Dusty" Foggo, a not-too-senior Agency officer whose career was mostly spent in what had been called the CIA's "Directorate of Administration." (The name has changed several times over the years, but the role of providing support for the Agency's worldwide operations has remained essentially the same.)

The men and women of the DA (now known as the

Directorate of Support) are miracle workers. It is hard enough providing logistical support to any government agency overseas. To be able to do it for a clandestine organization such as the CIA requires skill, imagination, and guts that are rarely seen elsewhere. They are the best in the world at what they do and I am indebted to them for the excellent support they provided to me and the organizations I led during my time in the Agency.

Goss's crowd had somehow gotten to know Dusty during trips to visit CIA activities in Europe. Apparently Foggo excelled at providing logistical support to the congressional delegation and they remembered his can-do attitude when they had an important hole to fill.

I had run across Dusty a few times during my Agency career, mostly in Latin America. He had the reputation of someone who could get the job done, and I understand that he did superb work out of Europe supporting CIA's post-9/11 logistical requirements. He was known as a wheeler-dealer, but that is one of the reasons he got stuff done. While he was good at being a "fixer" there was little in his record to suggest he was the right guy to become the third-ranking person at the CIA. But the Goss crowd thought he would be loyal to them and started the ball rolling to bring him back from overseas to fill that critical role.

Once again, Agency security and counterintelligence officers reviewed the personnel file in preparation. And once again they found some disturbing things. Press accounts have subsequently reported that Dusty had a major anger management problem and was known to have associated with some people with less-than-sterling reputations. Apparently whatever it was, it was not sufficient to have him removed from the Agency. The chief of counterintelligence for the Agency briefed Goss's chief of staff, Pat Murray, on her concerns and found him hostile to the news. Murray told her that if any of this derogatory information about Foggo leaked to the media, he would hold *her* personally responsible. Murray and friends apparently assumed that the information about Kostiw's past had been leaked by current counterintelligence (CI) officials. What they didn't understand was that even though personnel matters are handled discreetly within the Agency, there inevitably were scores of (mostly former) Agency officers who would have known about the reasons behind Kostiw's 1981 departure from the CIA. Once the announcement appeared in the media about Goss's picks, an announcement that Goss's team issued themselves, it wouldn't take long before someone would recall incidents involving the uniquely named former case officer and express their views on whether someone with his past was a good choice to hold the number-three position at the CIA in the future.

The counterintelligence chief was somewhat taken aback by the vehemence of Murray's views and recounted the discussion with her boss, Mike Sulick, the number-two person in the Directorate of Operations. Mike is a crusty, Bronx-born, seasoned intelligence hand who had served in some of the most challenging operational assignments the Agency could offer, particularly in Soviet-dominated Eastern Europe. Sulick studied Russian language and literature at Fordham and eventually earned a Ph.D. from CCNY. He is a no-nonsense kind of guy and an excellent intelligence officer. Mike walked down the hall to tell Murray that he didn't appreciate one of his officers being threatened like that.

There are a couple of versions of how the conversation that followed went down. None of them suggest it went well. It ended with Murray and Sulick shouting at each other and Mike telling the chief of staff something along the lines of his not willing to be treated like some low-level "Hill puke."

Murray, a former high-level Hill puke, took offense. Shortly thereafter, Murray told some version of the story to Goss and convinced him that they needed to call in Sulick's boss, Steve Kappes, the head of the clandestine service, the "DDO," and tell him he must fire or reassign Sulick.

Clearly they didn't know Kappes well. A by-the-book, straitlaced former Marine, Steve had a strong sense of loyalty to the Agency and his subordinates. Being ordered to cashier his deputy by Murray, a lawyer whose CIA experience at that point totaled something short of five weeks, was clearly a nonstarter. All this was happening a few days after President Bush had narrowly won reelection, and the Gosslings appeared to feel empowered to clean house at the CIA. The collision between them and Kappes and Sulick seemed destined to end up with the worst possible result.

While I heard the heavy thuds from the seventh floor while the elephants wrestled with each other, I didn't think it was something that would affect me. One night in early November, after a typically arduous day in CTC, I had fallen into my bed exhausted and was just beginning to doze off around 10:30 p.m. when the phone rang. It was not unusual for me to get calls at all hours of the day and night from the duty officer in the Agency's operations center, but this was something else. Dusty Foggo, the new executive director, was on the line insisting, without further explanation, that I meet him in his office right away. Wearily, I got dressed, jumped into my car, and drove to headquarters.

When I got there, Foggo was waiting for me in his office across the hall from the DCI's executive suite. He quickly got to the point. He explained to me that Kappes and Sulick would likely quit or be fired in the next few days. Goss and company wanted to be ready with a replacement as head of the clandestine service if that happened. Dusty said the leading contender for the job was me. It hadn't dawned on me that that was what this was all about. In retrospect, I suppose it should have. But I was totally focused on my job in CTC.

"No. I don't want it," I responded instantly and with passion. I had three reasons. First, I told him that I felt strongly that Kappes and Sulick were outstanding career officers who had risen to the top of the clandestine service on the basis of merit and achievement. Their sudden removal following a confrontation with a newly arrived, highly political staffer would be seen by the rank and file as a dangerous precedent. Such an action could undermine the professionalism and integrity of the clandestine service. There was still time, I told him, for Goss to fix the problem if he just dealt with Kappes and Sulick directly. Second, I had a job, a very important one, as head of CTC. I was needed in CTC and there were things I still hoped to accomplish, such as finding UBL and finishing off the remnants of the al-Qa'ida organization that had attacked us on 9/11.

Beyond that, my third reason for not wanting the job was more practical. I had already decided that I was going to retire in the summer of 2005 (after, I hoped, cleaning up some of those remaining details, such as getting bin Ladin). Having already spent twenty-eight years in the clandestine service, I felt it would be soon time to start the next phase of my life. But Dusty wouldn't take no for an answer. He kept telling me that the Agency needed me in this time of crisis (I restrained myself from reminding him it was a crisis of the Gosslings' creation). Still, I wasn't buying it.

I held to my answer of "no thanks." Dusty asked me to think about it and not to make any firm decisions. I wearily agreed to do so and headed home for the second time that day.

The first thing the next morning I reached out to Steve Kappes and told him of my conversation with Dusty. "They offered me your job," I told him, "but I said no." I explained my rationale. Steve was still my boss. I felt that I owed it to him. Steve thanked me but didn't say anything else.

Tension on the seventh floor continued to build for the rest of the week. The timing could not have been worse. On Friday, November 12, the Agency's highly respected deputy director, John McLaughlin, announced his plan to retire, in what he called a "purely personal decision." It was no secret inside the building, however, that John had little confidence in the team that Goss had brought with him. Few of us did.

That same day, Kappes told Goss that he would not fire or reassign Sulick as Murray demanded. If the order stood, he told Goss, Kappes would quit and walk out the door with Mike. Goss refused to overrule Murray but asked Kappes to spend the weekend thinking over the situation in hopes that he would find a way to stay on.

As I mentioned earlier, one of the complaints that the Goss-lings had when they arrived, and one of the things they vowed to fix, was what they saw as an excessive amount of leaking to the press from inside the CIA. In many cases, the information that they blamed the Agency for leaking most likely came from other parts of government. But in some instances they were right. This was one of them.

News of the impending departure of Kappes and Sulick rocketed around the CIA headquarters and to Agency field stations around the world. Before the day was out reporters had gotten wind of the exchange and we had the bizarre situation of news organizations over the weekend speculating about personnel moves going on inside America's secret intelligence headquarters. "What will happen on Monday?" they asked. "Will they stay or will they go?"

The dysfunction of CIA senior personnel politics played out in the nation's media over the weekend. Suddenly everyone was analyzing the management turmoil at the CIA. It became a partisan issue as well. Senator Jay Rockefeller (D-WV) told reporters that Goss's decision "to take with him several staff with reputations for partisanship was very troubling, and now he faces rumors of a partisan purge at the CIA." Representative Jane Harman, the senior Democrat on the HPSCI, appeared on CBS News' *Face the Nation* and criticized the "highly partisan, inexperienced staff" that Goss had brought to Langley, saying, "Many of us worked with that staff in the House. Frankly, on both sides of the aisle in the committee, we were happy to see them go."

John McCain, the senior senator from Arizona, took an opposite point of view, telling the *New York Times* that the upheaval at the Agency was "absolutely necessary." He said, "One thing that has become abundantly clear, if it wasn't already, is that this is a dysfunctional agency, and in some ways a rogue agency."

Goss supporters were active with the media, too, portraying Kappes and Sulick as part of a rebellious Agency staff unwilling to accept leadership from those above them and anxious to bury evidence of their own past malfeasance.

Having the weekend to think matters over did nothing to change Kappes's and Sulick's minds. They announced to their employees on Monday morning that that day would indeed be their last at the CIA. The announcement, although anticipated for a few days, hit the headquarters like a bombshell. I went upstairs to their offices on the seventh floor but found a line of well-wishers stretched far down the hall. There must have been several hundred people there to extend heartfelt farewells. The line was so long I eventually gave up and went back to work in CTC.

Waiting for me was a note to call Dusty right away. He pressed me for an answer to the question, would I accept the job that Kappes had just left? Dusty gave me the full sales treatment once again. I was torn. Signing on as the DDO probably meant committing to stay in government for another couple of years. Working with the Gosslings held little attraction, and I didn't want to advance my career at the expense of the misfortune of two fine officers, Kappes and Sulick, who had gotten cross-threaded with them.

I asked Dusty what his plan B was. Nobody goes into a situation like this without an alternative course of action if your initial one won't work. He admitted they did have a fallback plan, which was to bring back to the Agency a former senior operations officer who had retired some years before. Dusty gave me the name. It was someone who had been a fine officer back during the Cold War but a person totally unfamiliar with the environment we were operating in now. "This could be another personnel disaster," I thought to myself. I told him that I needed to call my wife and discuss it with her. I went back to my office and placed the call. Patti was supportive, as always. We talked about the pros and cons but eventually I told her that I thought I owed it to the rank-and-file members of the clandestine service, particularly those who at that very moment were serving in war zones, to take the job. I couldn't, in good faith, leave them without an experienced hand at the helm. Patti said she would support my decision no matter what.

I hung up and called Dusty to tell him I would take the job. "Great," he said. "Now we just need to get you cleared."

The approval process for being assigned the most senior jobs at the Agency involved a six-point check with different offices in the CIA, including the Office of Security and the Office of the Inspector General. The IG's office reminded the seventh floor of my troubles eight years earlier, which had resulted in my being fired from the Latin America Division. For the next eight to ten hours it looked as if I was about to be told that I was not suitable for the position I had very reluctantly agreed to accept. Late that evening I got a call at home telling me that Goss, after having been briefed on my earlier dust-up with the IG, had nonetheless signed off on my assignment.

If you had told me a quarter of a century earlier, when I was just entering on duty with the Agency, that someday I, a Puerto Rican–born kid who had spent most of his life outside the United States, would be head of America's premier clandestine service, I would have thought you were kidding. And if you had predicted that I wouldn't be particularly happy about how I got there, I would have known you were nuts.

With more than a little trepidation, late in the day on that Monday I began to move my things from my dark, windowless, ground-floor CTC office to a spacious, light-filled DDO suite on the CIA's seventh floor.

Suddenly I found myself at the top of the Agency, both figuratively and literally very, very far from where I had begun. The atmosphere throughout the building was incredibly tense. President Bush had only recently squeaked through a narrow reelection victory and the partisans around Goss made it clear that they felt they had a mandate to shake the Agency up.

I never found Goss, himself, to be captured by this score-settling mood. He remained often unaware of the actions being taken in his name.

The Gosslings had managed to recruit a few midlevel career Agency officers who felt empowered to kick ass and take names on behalf of their new masters. One such officer let it be known that anyone who was too closely associated with the past regime (meaning Tenet, McLaughlin, and Kappes, apparently) would be singled out for retribution. Unfortunately, there are more than a few jerks like that guy in any organization. I used to refer to them as *pendejos,* a Spanish slang word for which the politically correct translation is roughly "incompetent dumbass." This particular *pendejo* went so far as to say that he was keeping a list of individuals who needed to be reassigned from their senior jobs. A few months later, one of the Gosslings came to me and told me that they wanted this same list-keeper to be promoted well ahead of his peers to Senior Intelligence Service (SIS) rank. Making SIS is the equivalent of becoming a flag or general officer in the military. "It is not going to happen," I said. "To promote this guy, I would have to take SIS rank away from someone who had earned it." The decision to promote people within the Operations Directorate followed a very methodical process and I was not going to let some newcomer interfere and dictate to me how to run my organization.

In an odd way, I felt somewhat bulletproof. Given the ugly way the Gosslings had forced my predecessor to resign, they couldn't really afford to have another senior officer bail out as well. I had decided to take a stand on those things I believed were important to the directorate and not go to battle stations on issues of lesser importance. Because I was prepared to leave rather than cave on important stuff, I was blessed with being able to stand on principle.

One of my first decisions after becoming DDO was to pick a deputy. After all, Kappes and his deputy, Mike Sulick, departed as a duo. I selected Rob Richer, a crafty former Marine with extensive experience in the Middle East. Most recently Rob had been chief of the Near East Division and had worked closely with me in CTC. He had been heavily involved in Agency operations in Iraq, something that I had not had to pay much attention to when I had the counterterrorism account. The continuing mess in Iraq would be one of my major headaches as DDO, and Rob's depth of understanding of what we were up against nicely complemented my expertise elsewhere.

I knew Rob to be the kind of officer who got things done and the kind of guy you wanted by your side in a foxhole, whether a real one or the bureaucratic kind that you find in Washington. I purposely selected someone who was hard-nosed and would not shy away from a confrontation if one was necessary.

Given the turmoil created by the sudden departure of Kappes and Sulick, the pounding the Agency was taking from various panels and commissions, and the considerable damage done almost daily by leaks of sensitive information, the feeling in the Directorate of Operations was that we were under siege and fighting for our lives.

When you are under attack it is easy to become totally consumed by the crisis du jour. But I felt it was essential that we worry not only about the wolves nearest our sled, but also about those just over the horizon. We set about building a five-year strategic plan that would put us in a position to deal effectively not only with the threats of terrorism or the security situation in Iraq and Afghanistan but also with challenges posed by Iran, North Korea, China, Russia, and others.

The so-called peace dividend of the early nineties, followed by the intense focus on counterterrorism post-9/11, had left the clandestine service badly weakened. I felt it was critical that we become a truly global intelligence service once again. We needed a plan to reopen stations that had been closed in the past decade, pay attention to emerging threats, and come up with a strategic plan that would make us a strong, vibrant, and relevant organization.

Rob Richer met with our division chiefs for months hammering out such a plan. When we had a document that we felt accurately reflected the path we wanted to take, I called back to headquarters every one of our chiefs of station. This was the first time in history that a worldwide conference of station chiefs had ever been held. Gathering them in the Agency's auditorium, the Bubble, we laid out the draft plan and invited vigorous debate. I told the assembled senior officers that if they had any concerns or disagreements that that was the time to express them. "Once you leave this conference," I told them, "this is not 'headquarters' plan' and this is not 'Jose Rodriguez's plan,' this is 'our plan.'" I had seen too many instances in the past in which people would pay lip service to headquarters direction and then anonymously snipe at it due to narrow parochial interests. There was a lot of spirited debate during that conference—every chief of station seemed to think that his or her country was the center of the universe. But in the end they came to agreement on a strategic plan. The plan was a good one; it continues to be the strategic plan of the NCS and is paying dividends to this day.

The intelligence community, Congress, and the White House came to recognize the limitations of a too-small clandestine service. As a result, President Bush authorized doubling the size of the clandestine service over a period of five years.

All this happened while we were dealing with a great deal of public skepticism. The CIA had taken quite a beating from the 9/11 Commission and also from another "blue ribbon" panel, the Silberman-Robb Commission, which had been appointed to look into why the intelligence community had gotten the WMD in Iraq story so wrong. On top of that the newly created director of national intelligence was being stood up with an uncertain mission and unclear lines of authority but with an apparent mandate to "go fix" what Congress and the administration saw as a broken intelligence apparatus.

When a major power player like the CIA appears to be wounded, all the other animals in the jungle (in this case, the DOD and the FBI, for example) start circling, trying to see if they can take advantage of any weakness. And the CIA was certainly wounded. It had gone from being the center of the intelligence universe to just one of the sixteen agencies that made up the intelligence community. Things were in danger of getting worse. Everyone had his own reorganization plan. Some elements of the Office of the Director of National Intelligence, supported by Senator Pat Roberts (R-KS), then chairman of the Senate Intelligence Committee, proposed splitting off the Directorate of Operations (my organization) and making it an independent agency known as the National Clandestine Service. From my time working at two "centers"—the Crime and Narcotics Center and the Counterterrorism Center at the CIA—I knew that the Agency's best work was done when operator, analyst, scientist, and support officer all worked together. Fracturing a working organization made no sense to me.

But I did see some advantage in cementing the DO's grasp on human intelligence collection. Too many other agencies were trying to get into the line of business we had been working on for over sixty years. They were trying to take over big chunks of our mission. There was something we could work with, however, in the WMD Commission report. While the commission was critical of many things, it did conclude that the CIA's Directorate of Operations was the gold standard for clandestine human intelligence operations for the United States and the world. Using this as a wedge, we began a series of negotiations within the administration and in particular with the DNI's office that led us in October 2005 to announce the establishment of the National Clandestine Service (NCS), which would remain part of the CIA. The CIA director was named the national human intelligence manager, and day-to-day responsibilities for running human intelligence was delegated to me as head of the NCS. I got an additional deputy, a two-star Marine general, whose job it was to coordinate human intelligence collection throughout government outside the CIA. The establishment of the new organization gave us a better view of what other agencies were doing and the capability and authority to step in when agencies started to work at cross-purposes. Most important, it gave us a leadership role in working together against the hardest of targets and sharing best practices with other intelligence collectors in the U.S. government. Many old-timers regretted that we gave up the title of DO—the Directorate of Operations. And despite the change in name, many of them insist on calling the organization "the DO" to this day. But I saw the change as important both because it presented an opportunity to be recognized not just as a "directorate" but as a "service" and also because it allowed us to gain more authority and undisputed claim to clandestine human intelligence supremacy in the U.S. intelligence community.

Grabbing this new authority wasn't easy. I ran into a lot of resistance from around the government, but surprisingly, nowhere was the resistance stronger than within the CIA. Dusty Foggo, the executive director, was particularly opposed to the move. I had the impression that he thought the Directorate of Operations was about to get too strong, particularly in comparison to its sister directorates at the Agency. "Here at the Agency," he explained to me, "we are four tribes of equal importance." As someone who spent his career in one of the other "tribes"—the support directorate—I could understand why Dusty would like to think that, but it made no sense to me.

"Wake up and smell the coffee!" I told him at one particularly heated meeting. "What makes the CIA special, what makes it unique, is its ability to send people out to collect clandestine human intelligence." I told him that lots of agencies had analysts, lots of them had scientists, and everybody had support staff. While I greatly respected and loved our analysts, scientists, and support officers and thought they were the best in government, what gave us our special cachet was the group of men and women who went out and stole secrets for the American government.

Eventually I won the argument and NCS was created. Dusty threw some bones to the other directorates by changing their titles. Previously the head of analysis, for example, was known as the "deputy director for intelligence" (a deputy to the CIA director, that is). Now he was to be known as "director for intelligence." If that made people happier, fine. I never saw the creation of the NCS as anyone else's loss, only a gain for the entire Agency.

While all this bureaucratic warfare was going on, the Agency and NCS were fighting a couple of real wars. The security situation in Iraq oscillated between bad and worse, and while we had some successes in the war against al-Qa'ida, the number of top AQ leaders being captured slowed to a trickle. While our concern about an imminent second-wave attack was slightly lessened, we remained convinced that al-Qa'ida was still working hard at pulling off another spectacular assault. The 2004 Madrid train bombings, July 2005 London subway attacks, Sharm el-Sheikh assault, and the November 2005 Amman, Jordan, hotel bombings gave plenty of cause for great concern.

But in the United States, for many people, the memories of 9/11 were starting to fade, and there was increasing political pressure to ratchet back our ability to interrogate any prisoners we might catch.

With all the attention the subject of interrogation was getting, it was inevitable that Congress would get involved. As part of the FY 2006 Defense Appropriations bill, various amendments were offered to try to restrict the ability of the executive branch to carry out certain forms of interrogation. Senator John McCain (R-AZ) proposed an amendment that eventually became the Detainee Treatment Act of 2005, which directed that no agency of the U.S. government, including the CIA, could subject people in its custody to "cruel, inhuman, or degrading treatment or punishment." It did not, however, define those terms. The amendment was passed by a vote of 90–9 in the Senate on October 5, 2005.

While the McCain amendment was being debated and after it passed, the DNI's office and the White House were leaning on CIA Director Goss to both continue the interrogation program and accept some new restrictions. At one point in late 2005 the NSC proposed some language to Goss that he accepted as a short-term holding position until he could consult those of us at headquarters. We convinced him that the proposal was unacceptable, and he wrote a very gutsy memo that he sent to National Security Advisor Steve Hadley. In the memo, dated December 23, 2005, he said that in his view the McCain amendment did not adequately defend CIA officers from potential prosecution, and in light of that, he suspended the use of all enhanced interrogation techniques. Goss told the White House that he could not in good faith allow CIA officers to be at risk of criminal prosecution for taking actions that appropriate legal authorities had previously told them were legal.

Goss's memo went over like a bomb at the White House. They believed they had a deal with him to keep pressing ahead with the detainee interrogation despite the risk presented by the McCain amendment, which had now become law. His relations with the DNI and the White House were never the same. A little more than four months later, on the morning of May 5, 2006, Goss was called to the White House and a short while later his resignation was announced. I do not know if this was the only cause for his dismissal, but it certainly contributed in a big way to his firing.

Goss made a number of gutsy decisions while CIA director.

At one point the inspector general wanted to single out individuals within the Agency's ranks and hold them personally responsible for shortcomings before 9/11. Goss, however, felt strongly that any shortcomings were institutional and collective and that it would be unfair to hang the responsibility of 9/11 mistakes on the shoulders of a few hardworking officers. It would have been much easier for him politically to take the opposite stance. This, too, was a courageous decision. Before he left the Agency for good, he and I had an opportunity to travel to the CIA's clandestine training facility, where a new class of case officers was graduating. Traditionally the CIA director is present to send off each class. In front of the new graduates, I surprised Goss by giving him "the Donovan Award," a medal honoring the founder of the CIA's World War II predecessor, the OSS. It is bestowed by the head of the Directorate of Operations and now the NCS on rare individuals who have done extraordinary work on behalf of the clandestine service. I told those present that Porter Goss had given his heart and soul to protect the men and women of the clandestine service. What I did not add was that he had also sacrificed his job in that effort.

Goss was succeeded by General Mike Hayden. A four-star air force officer, Hayden's arrival was cause for concern among some in our ranks. He came to us from being the number-two man in the DNI's office. Before that, he was head of the National Security Agency. It was easy to imagine that he might have been sent to the Agency to complete the job of putting us in our place and remove the "central" from the "Central Intelligence Agency." Those fears were unfounded.

Shortly after he came on board, I briefed him on the status of the clandestine service. I told him that we had just completed a banner year with considerable operational and bureaucratic success.

Over a period of three years we had more than doubled the

number of recruited assets (spies) in one of the most opaque targets on the planet. Elsewhere we had had remarkable success in penetrating hostile intelligence services and making inroads in collecting intelligence against foreign military powers and terrorist groups.

And yet, I told him, our potential momentum had been squandered by infighting within the Agency, where all the components were treated as equal, and by attacks from the outside (including from the organization he had just left—the DNI), in which other agencies were intent on eating our lunch.

Hayden proved to be the right man for the right time at the Agency. He studied the organization intensively and probed what he was told by us and others. As far as I could tell, he arrived with no preconceived notions. He listened carefully as I explained our most controversial operations, including the enhanced interrogation program, and after immersing himself in the details he became not only our defender but our champion. One of my greatest concerns, I told him, was that there seemed to be no "end game" for the detainees the CIA continued to hold. The general got it, and within a few months found a fix to a problem that had seemed to have no solution.

The Agency's relations with the White House and Congress were at an all time low, and Hayden suggested that he might be able to do the most good for the CIA by defending us "from the perimeter out." General Hayden's leadership was critical in reasserting our central role in the intelligence community and in our relationships with Congress and the White House.

Chapter 7

INVESTIGATIONS

During my three decades at the Agency we fought against totalitarian dictators, weapons proliferators, drug kingpins, and terrorists. But there were many times when it felt that we were spending more time battling so-called human rights organizations, congressional overseers, fame-seeking disgruntled former CIA employees, and our own inspector general's staff.

Going after terrorists and dictators was, in many ways, considerably more straightforward. It was clear our opponents were "the bad guys" and we were generally recognized as being on the side of good. But the second group—the gadflies and meddlers—had great success at convincing outsiders that *they* were fighting the good fight and that *we* were the source of evil.

You don't join the CIA if you have an overwhelming urge to be universally loved. But it is hard to explain how debilitating it can be to be constantly undermined and second-guessed.

My first significant experience with inquisition-by-overseer came during the mideighties when I was stationed in Central America. The CIA found itself embroiled in the so-called Iran-Contra controversy. Agency officers following the orders and fulfilling the desires of their political leaders found themselves at odds with ever-changing and often countervailing guidance from Congress. Actions that were encouraged one month were banned the next. Covert action programs designed to achieve laudable goals, such as stopping drug traffickers, undermining terrorists, and promoting democracy, were painted as rogue actions by politicians who periodically disagreed with our methods but not the desired results. CIA officers found themselves caught in the middle. If they moved cautiously they were called "risk-averse" by their bosses. If they moved aggressively they were called cowboys and even "criminals" by politicians and prosecutors anxious to score points against their rivals. To top matters off, tactics that were deemed perfectly appropriate for a period of time suddenly became off-limits due to changes in the mood of Congress.

In November 1986, I was working in El Salvador when we got word that William J. Casey, the director of Central Intelligence, was coming to pay us a visit. Normally the senior Agency officer in country would be in charge of hosting such a high-level visitor, including social events. My boss had just arrived in country, however, and didn't yet have a home suitable for throwing an event for the visiting DCI. So Patti and I volunteered to put on a dinner for Casey, his entourage, and select senior U.S. and Salvadoran officials. We could not help but notice that Casey appeared unwell. He struggled, not always successfully, to stay awake during the dinner. While at our home he received a call on a PRT-250, one of the earliest satellite phones then in use by the Agency. Casey's staff back at headquarters informed him that the Iran-Contra story was about to break in the press and summoned him urgently back home to deal with the mess. The director's staff quickly bundled him up and headed back to Washington. A few months later, on December 11, just hours before he was to testify before Congress, Casey collapsed in his office as a result of what was later revealed to be a stroke and brain tumor. He resigned from the Agency six weeks later and died in May 1987.

The brouhaha over Iran-Contra seemed to launch a thousand investigations. As with so many scandals, it was made worse by the fact that it happened on the eve of a presidential election. A group of investigators descended on San Salvador to dig into the matter. Quite fortunately, my boss had kept me out of much of the most controversial aspects of support for the Contras.

El Salvador had suffered a devastating earthquake in October 1986. Nearly fifteen hundred people had been killed, and much of the city's infrastructure was in ruins. The Agency's offices were unusable, and we had four officers crammed into a makeshift space inadequate for one. It was in this temporary workspace that IG investigators elected to grill me on what I knew about Iran-Contra. There was no privacy in our cramped quarters, and my colleagues couldn't help but eavesdrop on my whole interview. To this day my former boss enjoys telling what he heard. The IG interrogator asked question after question and I (honestly) kept saying: "I don't know." In frustration my inquisitor said, "You don't know much, do you?" To which I replied, "I don't know shit, man!"

Unfortunately, some of my former bosses, mentors, and colleagues did. Many of them, unfairly in my view, paid the price for taking actions that their superiors asked of them. The Latin America Division of the CIA was devastated, as some of our best officers were made scapegoats in Iran-Contra and a series of other largely trumped-up investigations, which continued through the early nineties. Among the officers were Jim Adkins and Jack McCavitt, two highly professional officers of high integrity and sterling reputation, who were mentors and friends of mine. Their premature departures were losses to the Agency and to me personally.

It was that environment that I walked into in 1995 when, at the request of CIA Director John Deutch, I became chief of the LA Division. A highly respected former chief of LA had been fired, and others retired under black clouds of controversy. The IG had recommended disciplinary action against more than a score of other division officers. Deutch had fired a number of the most popular and respected officers. In a meeting in "the Bubble," he told assembled remaining LA Division officers that he wanted them to be operationally aggressive and go out and take chances. The response was openly derisive laughter. In a show of solidarity for some of the fired officers, many LA Division officers began to wear black armbands in the headquarters or black bands across their ID badges.

It took all my skills as a leader to lift the sense of gloom in the division. But slowly, I was starting to make progress. Officers in headquarters and out in the field started to put the past behind them and regain a spring in their step. We had important work to do and some very talented people with whom to work.

Then one day in early 1997 I got a call from my superiors on the seventh floor regarding a new investigation that was being launched by the Inspector General's Office. That is never a good sign. I wondered which one of my people, spread from Washington to the tip of South America, had run afoul of the IG. Turns out, it was me.

My boss told me that someone had complained that I had inappropriately intervened on behalf of a drug dealer in a country in my region. It took a while after hearing the allegation to figure out what he was talking about. A year or so earlier, soon after I had taken my current job, I got a call from a friend of mine informing me that a mutual boyhood friend of ours had been arrested and imprisoned in a Caribbean nation on drug charges. The local police entered his now-empty home and helped themselves to the contents. They even stole his car. Of far greater concern, however, were reports that the police were brutally beating their prisoner. My friend asked me if I could do anything to stop the mistreatment of our buddy, whom I had not seen in a very long time. I told him that if our friend indeed had gotten himself mixed up in the drug trade, he deserved to be in prison. I spent much of my Agency career fighting drug traffickers, and the notion that someone I knew might be contributing to the drug epidemic was distressing to me.

Still, the thought of officials beating him was disturbing. Many officers in my division had been punished in the recent past for not intervening when Latin American officials mistreated detainees. So I agreed to look into the matter.

I called the senior CIA officer in the country in question. My friend was not unknown to him. He had provided some logistical support for our station there. I told the station chief: "Look, if Hector (not his real name) is in the drug trade, he deserves to get busted. But please check with the local intelligence service and ask them not to beat the man and not to steal from him. If he is guilty, bring him to trial. But don't abuse him."

The station chief did just that and the local authorities listened. I was told the beatings stopped. Contacting local authorities and asking them to treat prisoners with basic decency is something that the CIA insists on.

Far from being a drug trafficker, Hector turned out to be a recreational user of cocaine. Eventually he was released without charges. When he went home, many of his belongings, including his stolen car, had miraculously returned. I thought nothing more about it and to this day have never spoken with Hector, my former friend, again.

Sometime after Hector's incarceration, a CIA officer in our station with a less-than-stellar record found himself in trouble. His bosses discovered he had been condescending and abusive toward the local intelligence service.

Our station chief sent an "eyes only" cable to me reporting on the performance problems of his subordinate and asking what should be done. Despite the title "eyes only," such cables were automatically seen by several people, including my boss, the DDO, Dave Cohen. As soon as Cohen saw the report, he directed that the officer be immediately recalled to headquarters. That pretty much ended the officer's career (which frankly was going nowhere anyway).

The guy being recalled apparently assumed that I was the one who had ordered that his career be terminated. In fact, I had not. But feeling aggrieved, he proceeded to seek retribution. The troubled officer contacted the IG's office and said that he was being singled out for retribution because, he claimed, he had told local authorities of intelligence that led to Hector's arrest. This was nonsense. I had no idea then or now whether he had anything to do with Hector's being singled out for investigation. In the world of the IG, however, a charge is as good as evidence, and an investigation was launched.

I later learned that, just to make sure he got even with me, the officer also reported to the Drug Enforcement Agency that I had forced the station to intervene on behalf of a druggie. I knew the allegations were absurd, so I figured if I laid out the facts, the IG would do its thing and eventually the problem would go away. The IG did its thing all right, but it was I who would end up going away.

After several months of investigation the IG staffer called and asked me to come to his office at the new headquarters building, adjacent to the "original" headquarters building where my staff and I worked. When I got there, he closed the door. "I want to share with you my draft report and get your reaction," he said. I sat down and started to read the lengthy report. My jaw dropped. When I finished, I slowly pushed the report back across the desk and told him: "I don't know who this guy is you are writing about. It isn't me. It isn't me!" He didn't get what I was saying. I explained that he was dead wrong and that he had accepted almost every bit of bullshit given to him by the disgraced former employee of our station. He told me I could submit a written rebuttal. I went home and spent an entire weekend crafting a passionate defense of my honor. On Monday I gave my paper to the IG rep but later learned that it had been a waste of time. Despite my protestations, the IG report was forwarded, virtually unchanged, to my boss, the DDO. By this time the CIA had undergone yet another change of leadership. George Tenet had become the sixth DCI in the past decade. When he came aboard he brought Jack Downing, a highly respected former case officer, out of retirement to be DDO. Jack was an old cold warrior, who spoke both Russian and Chinese and had served with great distinction in Moscow and elsewhere.

A somewhat humorless former Marine, Downing walked into my office carrying a copy of the IG report. He said he wanted to hear my side of the story firsthand. I was delighted to tell it. Apparently I was more delighted than he was to hear it, because a few minutes into my animated self-defense I looked to him and noticed that Downing had fallen asleep. I did not take that as a good omen.

When CIA officers are subject to adverse IG reports or otherwise get into trouble, the common solution is generally to hold an "accountability board." A panel of senior officers is assembled to read the report and recommend some action. The deck is often stacked. The IG has a phalanx of investigators to build a case against you. I was not allowed to be present; they had only my written rebuttal to make my defense.

The case officer who was my accuser had done a good job of sabotaging my career. Not only were the allegations serious, that a senior CIA official was protecting a drug dealer who was a personal friend, but the timing could not have been worse. The Agency had just been through a searing controversy in which a California newspaper, the *San Jose Mercury News,* had reported that the CIA was behind the crack cocaine epidemic in Los Angeles in the 1980s. The allegation was absurd and was debunked by numerous official and unofficial investigations. But it was accepted as fact by a number of harsh Agency critics, including Congresswoman Maxine Waters, who never met a conspiracy theory about the CIA that she wasn't ready to believe.

The stars were not aligned in my favor. The station chief whom I had asked to contact the local officials to request they stop beating their prisoner apparently later told the IG, "I thought Jose's request was inappropriate." He never said "boo" about it to me at the time.

The accountability board didn't have a lot of options, especially when confronted with an IG report that concluded that I had displayed "a remarkable lack of judgment." I knew some of the folks on the accountability board. It must have been very difficult for them to sit in judgment of one of their colleagues.

Jack Downing came down to my office on a late October morning to deliver the verdict. This time he stayed awake throughout our session. "You are being relieved of your duties as chief of the Latin America Division," he said. The Agency would find some place to stash me, Downing explained, until they could figure out what other assignment I might be eligible for.

As it turned out, on the calendar that morning was a long-scheduled conference of all the chiefs of station under my division. A couple of dozen senior officers from throughout the division were in town for meetings. I might as well finish up those meetings, Jack said, before cleaning out my desk.

One of the main events of any chiefs-of-station conference is for the visitors to be addressed by the DDO. It is a chance for them to hear about the status of the directorate from the top man in the clandestine service. Downing was on the agenda to speak to this group, and he figured it was necessary to break the news to them that their division chief, this Rodriguez guy, was on his way out.

Before they could hear it elsewhere, I quickly informed my own headquarters staff about my firing. As far as I know, however, none of the station chiefs had any idea that I was even under investigation, let alone about to be fired, until Downing walked into their meeting.

They were a happy group that morning gathered in the Latin America Division conference room down the hall from my office. Jack greeted them and, with me standing at his side, in a matter-of-fact tone went through the allegations contained in the IG report and concluded by saying that for those reasons I was no longer chief, LA. One of the officers present later told me that this was the most surreal meeting she had ever attended in her long Agency career. "I kept wondering," she later told me, "does Downing not see Jose in the room?" Jack's explanations did not go over well with those in the room, who were gratifyingly loyal to me. He got peppered by increasingly hostile questions. His answers did little to satisfy the crowd. Some wondered whether there was a curse hanging over LA Division. Its most senior officers kept getting shot out of the saddle. Downing's briefing went over so badly, in fact, that later during the multiday meeting Jack came back to meet the group a second time to again try to explain the action.

When Downing left, I walked to the front of the room and gave a very brief synopsis of what my actions truly were and why I had taken them. I explained that I had made a single call to protect someone who was being brutally beaten. "Knowing what I know now," I said, "including the damage that my actions have caused to my career, I would do exactly the same thing again." My remarks were much more warmly received than were Downing's.

I did not blame Downing for my firing from LA. In a way his hands were also tied by the IG's recommendations and the decision of the accountability board. I later learned that in addressing a different chief-of-stations conference, he expressed regret at having to remove me from my position and described me as one of the best leaders in the directorate. Years later, when I had Jack's job, I invited him back to headquarters for briefings on the state of the organization. I treated him with the respect that he had earned as a leader and legendary cold warrior.

Eventually, George Tenet, the new DCI, came down to address the group. He had been briefed on how badly Downing's earlier sessions had gone. "Don't worry," George said. "Jose will be all right." Few in the room, including me, believed him, but as it turned out, he was right.

We had previously scheduled a party at my home that evening for all the visiting officers. Patti and I were not going to let a little thing like my being fired stand in the way of a good party. It happened to be Halloween and Patti had the house decorated appropriately. She added one final touch—a cardboard tombstone placed with the inscription: "RIP Jose." My (now former) officers got in the spirit, too, bringing with them a large pumpkin with the words "We love you, man" carved in it.

I appreciated the sentiment and welcomed all the support I could get, because it appeared to me that my Agency career, which had been on a rapid, upward trajectory for the past twenty-two years, had just crashed and burned. Years later I would take note of the irony that in 1997 I was fired for trying to stop people from beating a petty criminal, and a decade later I came under criminal investigation for my involvement with the harsh, but legal and authorized, interrogation of some mass murderers.

If there is one constant about negative IG reports, it is that they always seem to leak. This one was no different. A few weeks after I got the ax, someone dropped the details of my removal from LA Division on the *Los Angeles Times*. The leaker provided the reporter considerable detail on the allegations, including my full name. With some difficulty the Agency's press office convinced the newspaper not to disclose my identity, pointing out that doing so might be a violation of federal law. They also stressed that the Agency did not believe I had intervened to save a drug dealer, only that I was trying to make sure a former friend was not mistreated. These details got lost ten years later when I was in the news again, this time over the destruction of videotapes of the interrogation of some senior al-Qa'ida members. By then any nuance had disappeared, and some media outlets reported that I had once been severely sanctioned for protecting a "drug kingpin."

Despite the damage to my career and ego from having been fired, I managed to survive. I spent the next eight months working on a project with the office of security, trying to resolve the cases of Agency officers who were in professional limbo due to overly cautious polygraphers and overly aggressive FBI investigators. In the aftermath of the scandal over Aldrich Ames (a CIA case officer who reportedly passed a polygraph but turned out to have been working for the Russians), the default position at the CIA was to place many innocent people under suspicion of wrongdoing. Scores of loyal case officers had a black cloud of suspicion over their heads. They were not allowed to perform significant duties, were deemed unassignable to new positions, and lived with the knowledge that at any moment they might be fired in disgrace or arrested.

During my time working with security, we were able to come up with steps that forced the FBI to make decisions and either act on people they thought were security risks or lift the cloud and let them go back to work. CIA security personnel worked diligently with me to help fix an untenable situation. The number of people in limbo, called "hall walkers" at the Agency because they couldn't perform any of the Agency's real jobs, diminished sharply. I had more than a little sympathy for those who were falsely accused and felt good about being able to help many in those circumstances resolve their cases. By no means was the nightmare of false accusation ended, however.

Brian Kelley was the most extreme example of security run amok. A retired air force officer who had become an outstanding counterintelligence officer at the CIA, Brian came under suspicion of being a Russian mole in the late 1990s. The FBI confronted him and refused to believe his denials. They harassed him mercilessly. The Bureau interviewed his elderly mother, his children, and other family members and told them that without question he was a spy. After being suspended from work for almost two years, during which time his phones were tapped and he was routinely followed, the Bureau discovered they had the wrong man. The real Russian mole was Brian's Vienna, Virginia, neighbor, FBI agent Robert Hanssen.

In my next job, in Mexico, I had a few run-ins with headquarters-based counterintelligence officers whose zealousness in dismissing potential hard-target recruits based on old assumptions and a risk-averse mind-set cost the CIA opportunities to recruit foreign agents who wanted to volunteer information to us. Despite those incidents, I believe counterintelligence must play a critical role in the operation of an intelligence agency. Any organization that acts as if it cannot be penetrated by its enemies or that thinks its information is invulnerable is setting itself up for a huge fall.

All the investigations I was party to during my first twenty-five years at the CIA would pale in comparison to what would come next.

• • •

It is fair to say that in the days immediately after 9/11, when I first reported to CTC, the Agency's counterterrorism efforts were frenzied and chaotic. We were flooded with added people, empowered with new authorities, and, almost overnight, swamped with a boatload of cash to enable us to carry out our critical mission.

While no one wanted to stand in our way in our efforts to smash al-Qa'ida, it was perfectly logical that Agency leadership wanted to make sure that we were using our vastly expanded resources wisely. Almost simultaneously with the arrival of our new assets came a platoon of auditors from the Inspector General's Office. That was understandable. Give an outfit a billion dollars or so and you have a right to want to make sure they are spending it well.

The IG Office has three main activities: audits, to make sure you are using your dollars correctly; inspections, periodic efforts to verify that rules and regulations are being followed; and investigations, when there have been allegations of wrongdoing and the IG wants to dig into the charges.

For the IG in the post-9/11 period, the auditors were the advance landing party in CTC. Once they were aboard, their colleagues followed and, rather than being visitors, they took up permanent residence.

An outsider might say, "So what's the problem? As long as you and your colleagues are not doing anything wrong, what does it matter that the IG staff is embedded with you?" Imagine you are playing football. But the referees are focused only on your team, and not only do they watch you during the plays, but they are also in your huddle, in the locker room, and on the practice field just itching to throw a flag. Or it is like taking a motorcycle out on the road and knowing that the cops are salivating to give you a ticket. But the traffic cop is not up the road hiding behind a billboard, he is in a sidecar attached to your bike. Sure, you are smart enough to keep it under the speed limit, but every time you swerve to avoid a pothole you risk being cited for reckless driving.

The constant presence of IG staff within CTC became a fact of life for us. I had monthly meetings with John Helgerson, the IG, during which we compared notes on the many efforts his staff had on delving into the work of mine. For the most part ours was not an adversarial relationship.

The more access the IG staff got, the more they wanted, and I tried to be helpful. I ordered that IG staffers be given access to some of CTC's most sensitive materials, including the database with operational traffic coming in from the black sites with the full details of information obtained from our most senior al-Qa'ida detainees and a complete description of the techniques used to acquire it.

While all this was going on, the IG's staff was also working on an investigation into how 9/11 happened. Their investigation was parallel with and separate from the other intense reviews such as the Joint Congressional Inquiry and the 9/11 Commission. The people who were most critical to answering questions for those investigations were our most valuable CTC officers, who also were in the fight against al-Qa'ida going forward. They were constantly being pulled away from their efforts to stop the next attack to look back at how the last one had happened. While this was emotionally and physically draining for them, it was one of my leadership challenges to explain to them that both efforts—looking back and looking forward—were critical and needed our full support.

There are lots of problems with IG investigations. I know that, having been personally slammed in a few of them, my criticisms will be viewed by many with skepticism. But only those who have been subjected to the special scrutiny of the

IG staff, an experience that one of my colleagues described as like being "a test dummy at a proctologist's college"—can fully understand.

To be brutally honest, one of the biggest problems with the CIA's IG staff is that the Agency's best and brightest don't usually seek assignments there. If you are a fast-tracking analyst, scientist, or case officer, the last thing you want to do with your career is take a several-year-long timeout to second-guess your former colleagues who are doing the real work. People assigned to the IG staff are generally "on rotation"—that means they are loaned to the IG from other parts of the Agency. Who gets encouraged to take an assignment there? Mostly people whose absence at the home office will not be missed. This sets up a potential, almost inevitable, ugly clash. You take people whose careers have been not stellar and you ask them to rate and examine their former colleagues. It is like middle school, where you give a few kids a reflective vest and badge and make them crossing guards. They can't wait to start blowing the whistle on their more popular friends.

In addition to bringing in staffers who have chips on their shoulders, the IG also brought in people who had noticeable agendas. For example, one of the most senior officers on the staff was married to one of the Agency's most vitriolic external critics.

It is bad enough that the personnel were flawed, but the process used by the IG's reporting was also stacked against their targets. Since 1989, the CIA inspector general has been a "statutory IG." That means that he (and, so far, it has always been a "he") is appointed by the president and confirmed by the Senate. He is independent and does not view himself as working for the CIA director. He can and does report his findings directly to Congress. The Agency's director has the power, though rarely exercised, to restrain the IG from releasing some particularly sensitive information. Doing so runs the risk of being accused of a cover-up, however, so the IG is immensely powerful.

As I learned when I was first the target of the IG during my time in the Latin America Division, while the person under investigation has the right to respond to charges, the IG is under no obligation to include that response in his report. When the IG's (often flawed) report goes to Capitol Hill, the written rebuttal from the people he has skewered rarely goes with it. Sometimes the IG's report is declassified and made public and again, the self-defense provided by those who are the targets almost never reaches the public eye.

Some people argue that a statutory IG is a violation of the constitutional separation-of-powers provision. You have the IG, essentially an employee of Congress, sitting in executive branch meetings, embedded in executive branch operations, and responsible for the most part only to his masters on the Hill.

During my time in CTC and as head of the National Clandestine Service, the IG's staff produced numerous badly flawed reports. But some of the worst damage done by the IG's staff came from activities that themselves deserved investigation. But who audits the auditors? Who inspects the inspectors? And who investigates the investigators?

In 2004 and 2005, the Agency became increasingly alarmed about stories that appeared in the mainstream media with sensitive details of our detention and interrogation programs. Some of the details that leaked were known to only a relative handful of people in the U.S. government—almost all of whom were at the CIA. People at the Agency like to think that most damaging leaks of sensitive information come from

Congress, the White House, or some other agency that has a dispute with the CIA. But in this case it was pretty obvious that the culprit or culprits were in-house.

Concern about this problem came to a crescendo about the time Porter Goss and his team arrived at the CIA. One of Goss's mandates was to try to stop the leaks coming from Langley, and I fully supported him. Goss's number-three man, Dusty Foggo, demanded that the Agency's office of security get to the bottom of the mess. Some of Goss's senior staffers guessed that the leaks might be coming out of the IG's office. (What gave them that idea, I do not know.) Foggo told the security staff to make sure the IG was scrutinized. (It must have been somewhat surreal for the security folks, since something that neither the Goss staff nor I knew then was that at the very same time, the IG staff was working with the Department of Justice and CIA security on an investigation of Foggo. Dusty would later be indicted and plead guilty in a contracting fraud case and be sentenced to thirty-seven months in federal prison.)

I knew nothing about Dusty's problems at the time—I simply recognized the urgent need to plug the leaks coming from within the Agency on some of our most sensitive programs. Very few people were "read in" on the programs in question. And many of those people were quite senior, so no one was out of suspicion—including me. The office of security built a matrix of the range of people who were known to be aware of some of the most sensitive details that had leaked.

I agreed that the best place to start was to go to each of those people and ask them to submit to a "single issue" polygraph exam. Agency officers are accustomed to periodic polygraph tests. When first entering the Agency and periodically thereafter you are subjected to lengthy in-depth sessions strapped to a machine designed to determine if you are being truthful when answering a broad range of security and lifestyle-related questions. But in this case there was just one issue: Have you shared information about the CIA's interrogation and detention program with anyone unauthorized to receive it? The only way to ensure that we didn't inappropriately target anyone based on preconceived notions about who might be responsible was to start at the very top and polygraph the most senior people who were knowledgeable about the program.

I volunteered to be polygraphed, as did Porter Goss. Some twenty to thirty people, including the IG himself, were put "on the box," as it is called in the Agency. The polygraph (widely and incorrectly known as a "lie detector") is not perfect. It can generate false-positive reports. The people in security were worried. "Oh God, what if the director has a false positive on this?" they asked themselves. Fortunately, neither Goss, nor I, nor the others in the first group showed deception on the test.

Security then expanded their search to a slightly wider range of people—somewhat lower on the totem pole but still fully read in on the program. Four or five people had trouble with their polygraph exams. Some on Goss's staff wanted to immediately brief Congress about the status of the investigation, including the names of the possible suspects. Fortunately, that wasn't done, because, as sure as night follows day, the names of some of the suspected leakers would have leaked, ruining their careers. We weren't yet sure enough about any of them.

With the set of potential candidates, however, security began to drill down. Soon they found hard evidence that one of them, a senior official in the Inspector General's Office, had been in regular telephone contact with reporters, including Dana Priest of the *Washington Post*. The Agency has strict rules about unauthorized contact with the media. Even without passing on classified information, talking to the media without approval is a violation of Agency regulations and can get you fired. My understanding is that at first she denied any contact with the media. When presented with evidence to the contrary, she admitted that there had been some discussion but nothing sensitive. The polygraph indicated otherwise. Eventually the officer revealed she had had discussions that seemed to me well beyond any reasonable explanation. She blamed the reporter for tricking her into confirming things that she had not planned to discuss.

In a meeting in the director's office with other senior officials, Dusty Foggo recommended (tongue in cheek, I hope) that the officer be taken out to the Agency's courtyard and hanged as an example to others. While that was considerably more extreme than what I favored, and although she claimed to have violated no law, I believed that prosecution was certainly called for. Press accounts said that the officer was later fired and marched out of the building in disgrace. In the end she was allowed to retire (which she was about to do anyway), so the price of betraying her oath was small indeed. I am at a loss to explain why she wasn't prosecuted. There is always a calculus on the part of the government of avoiding going after leakers, because if you do so, much more information about sensitive programs may be exposed in the course of a trial. Nonetheless, letting someone escape with little, if any, sanction for such acts hardly provides a message of deterrence to those left behind.

Leaks like this person's did great damage to the CIA. They did damage to allied countries that volunteered to help us and saw their assistance repaid with exposure in the press. But the leaks also did great damage to the Office of the Inspector General. The IG Office was already vastly distrusted within the Agency because of its holier-than-thou attitude and the prosecutorial way they routinely treated fellow CIA employees. Now they had demonstrated that they could not be trusted with the secrets shared with them. The question arose: Who will watch the watchers?

The general disgust over the way the IG Office operated within the CIA led Agency director Mike Hayden in May 2007 to courageously order one of his senior advisors, Bob Dietz, to conduct a study of how the IG functioned. I say "courageously" because to many outsiders the IG is a sacred cow. The notion of questioning anything about the way the office performed its duties would cause outrage among those who treated IG pronouncements as holy writ.

Hayden wanted the review of the IG operation to be conducted quietly. He simply wanted to know if the many complaints he was hearing from his workforce about them were well-founded.

Naturally, the existence of the internal inquiry leaked. The *New York Times* reported that the review had caused "anxiety and anger in Mr. Helgerson's office and aroused concern on Capitol Hill." Dietz had been general counsel at the National Security Agency when Hayden was its director and was a trusted counselor to him at the CIA. An Agency spokesman told the *Times* that Hayden's goal was to help the IG staff "do its vital work even better."

At one point, after the four-month study was launched, John Helgerson, the IG, is said to have told senior Agency officials, "You have no idea how much toll this investigation has taken on my staff!" I'm sure my colleagues in CTC who had been under constant scrutiny from the IG for the past seven years shed some tears for the IG's staff.

In the end, as a result of Dietz's study, about fifteen procedural steps were implemented to try to restore trust in the IG process. Among them, Hayden ordered the establishment of an ombudsman whom Agency employees could go to if they felt unfairly treated by the IG. That was a long way from solving the problem, but it was a start.

When Dietz's study was completed, there was little fanfare.

Hayden asked Helgerson about sending it to Capitol Hill. Normally a strong proponent of congressional notification, Helgerson demurred, saying there was no need, since this was just "an internal matter." Oddly, most of the substance of Dietz's findings didn't leak. The fact that there was a study under way did get out—and when Congress heard about it, and realized that they had not been officially informed, quite predictably they went crazy.

The self-inflicted wounds we faced came not only from the IG staff. There were a number of self-proclaimed experts who spoke out through the press, made speeches, and wrote books that greatly clouded the public understanding of CIA operations post-9/11. Many of these critics came from inside the tent. The closer they could claim to have been to the scene of what they called a crime and the more loudly they denounced our actions, the more they were embraced by large segments of the media. I've already touched on some of these gadflies.

There was the former FBI agent who was involved during the early days after Abu Zubaydah was captured. He has declared himself a leading expert on radical Islam and convinced the media that, based on his native Arabic-speaking skills, he is one of America's leading experts on terrorism. The truth is that this former agent was not only held in low regard by the CIA officers with whom he worked, but also, as I understand it, fellow FBI colleagues were privately quite dismissive of his performance and attitude. While he had experience in other investigations, he has grossly exaggerated his role concerning his brief involvement in Abu Zubaydah's case and turned it into a manifesto about how he was always right and the CIA was always wrong on dealing with terrorists.

The former agent has mischaracterized both his role and

that of Agency officers and contractors in the early interrogation. Having provided his spin for years on background to various reporters and authors, he then "reluctantly" confirmed his own tale in appearances in the media and in a book. He has created quite a myth.

The most egregious of his many misstatements is that "we never got any actionable intelligence, comparatively to what we got before, when [the EITs] were going on." This absurd statement has been disputed by every CIA director and director of national intelligence since 9/11. It is made by a person who, after the summer of 2002, and before the first EIT was ever applied, was no longer even privy to what intelligence had been obtained from whom in the Agency's interrogation program. When back at FBI headquarters or in the field, he might have seen a subset of the intelligence derived from the detainees, but it would have been presented in such a fashion that it would not have been immediately discernible to him who the source was.

I don't want to give the impression that I am picking only on the FBI. The CIA also has several alumni of its own whose statements, media appearances, and books have subtracted from the sum of accurate knowledge on the Agency's interrogation program.

There was a midlevel Agency officer who was present in Pakistan when Abu Zubaydah was captured. He went on to convince the media that he had led the effort to get AZ, when, as I understand it, some say he was not even in the same city at the time of the takedown. After leaving the CIA, he somehow persuaded Hollywood to hire him as an advisor on the film *The Kite Runner.* When that movie was coming out in December 2007, he told people he was trying to build on his reputation and was considering writing a book about his life that could be made into a screenplay.

My love of horses goes back to my early childhood. Here I am sitting on our milkman's horse in Buga, Colombia. My father is behind me. My parents later learned that the milkman was an insurgent. *Rodriguez family photo*

As a young CIA officer in the early 1980s I was able to ride horses in a number of locations throughout Latin America, even reconnecting with someone from whom I took riding lessons as a boy, then-Captain Luis Garcia Meza of Bolivia. In 1980 Garcia Meza had taken over in a coup and had become the first narcodictator in the continent.

In 1986 I was working in El Salvador, where the Fidel Castro–inspired Farabundo Martí National Liberation Front (FMLN in Spanish) was conducting a violent civil war. Here we are helping distribute humanitarian aid in an area heavily controlled by the rebels.

CIA Director R. James Woolsey presented me the National Intelligence Distinguished Service Medal in 1994 for my work in Latin America during the early 1990s. I treasured this award because I was nominated for it by Ambassador Dean Hinton, who was known to be very demanding of intelligence officers.

In 1995 I led an Agency delegation to China to discuss counternarcotics cooperation. I was touched to hear that at a formal dinner our hosts planned to serve "rice and beans," a tribute, I thought, to my Hispanic heritage. Later my staff told me it was really "rice and bees."

George Tenet, then deputy director of Central Intelligence, presenting me with an Intelligence Community award in 1996.

Patti and I talk with former president George H. W. Bush at a September 1997 event at Blair House in Washington, D.C., marking the fiftieth anniversary of the establishment of the CIA. President Bush was CIA director when I entered on duty at the CIA in 1976.

With Patti at the celebration of the CIA's fiftieth anniversary—September 1997.

Our sons, Nic and Alec, at their grandfather's farm in Puerto Rico, December 1997.

Alec (middle), Nic, and I riding our horses in La Marquesa National Park on the outskirts of Mexico City, August 6, 2001. Just before our return to the United States.

A view from an Agency helicopter early in the war in Afghanistan.

A photo I took of a helicopter early in the Afghan war.

On a visit to Afghanistan in March 2002. We took care to try to blend in with the locals with our attire.

Afghan president Hamid Karzai hitched a ride on a CIA aircraft traveling from Tashkent, Uzbekistan, to Kabul, circa 2002.

As part of my duties as chief of CTC and later as head of the National Clandestine Service, I led many delegations to meetings with foreign intelligence services. I can't show the people on the other side of the table.

A family vacation in the Dominican Republic, December 2002.

My passion for riding horses and motorcycles extends to other forms of transport, too. This was a trip to Egypt in 2003.

No trip to Baghdad in 2004 was complete without a visit to one of Saddam Hussein's former "sex palaces"—where he used to entertain his mistresses.

On a trip to Yemen in 2004, I try out a Russian-made Dishka light machine gun.

Yemen had become a center of increased counterterrorism focus by 2004. Here I am mixing with some tribal elements.

Addressing Yemeni counterterrorism troops in 2004.

CIA Director General Mike Hayden and I at a luncheon hosted by General Ashfaq Kayani, then head of Pakistan's intelligence service, the ISI, in August 2006. Just a few days later, Kayani and I would make some critical decisions trying to stop those plotting to bring down aircraft with liquid explosives.

On a trip to Egypt in 2006, I met with Omar Suleiman, then head of Egypt's General Intelligence Service (EGIS).

Actor Robert De Niro learned how to pick locks for a scene in his 1988 movie, *Midnight Run*. Years later, I took him to a CIA facility where Agency officers have perfected the art.

the man behind the legend - the one and only Jose - a real leader rising to the challenge of old problems successfully and new problems boldly. I am in awe! Gratefully, Porter 7/06

CIA Director Porter Goss presented me with the "Directors Medal" on his departure. (I had previously received one from former DCI George Tenet.) The inscription on the back of the rarely awarded medal reads "Extraordinary Fidelity and Essential Service." *Official CIA photo*

General Mike Hayden, the tenth and final CIA director I worked for, presented me with my third "Directors Medal" when I stepped down as chief of the National Clandestine Service in August 2007 and prepared to retire. *Official CIA photo*

Jose - Many thanks for your work and your friendship, Mike Hayden

Patti and I at a farewell reception in my honor as I stepped down as chief of the NCS. Although I retired four months later, there was no retirement ceremony, because by that time I was under investigation by the Department of Justice.

An aerial shot of CIA headquarters. In the foreground is the "Original Headquarters Building" and to the rear is the "New Headquarters Building." ©2011 Greg E. Mathieson, Sr. / MAI

The seal of the CIA is embedded in the floor of the main lobby in the Original Headquarters Building in McLean, Virginia. No matter how many times I walked across it, the sight always gave me a thrill. ©2011 Greg E. Mathieson, Sr. / MAI

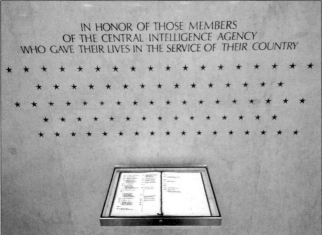

There is a "Wall of Honor" in the lobby of CIA headquarters on which a star is carved in marble to represent each officer who gave his or her life in the line of duty. When I first entered on duty with the CIA there were fewer than forty stars on the wall. Today there are more than one hundred. ©2011 Greg E. Mathieson, Sr. / MAI

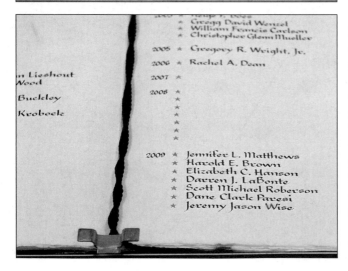

Below the stars carved in the wall is a book listing the fallen officers. Because of the secret nature of the work they did, often the names must be omitted. Those who remain undercover, even in death, are represented in the book by a star and a blank space where their name might have been inscribed. ©2011 Greg E. Mathieson, Sr. / MAI

At one point, I'm told, he sent an email to friends saying, "Hey everybody, watch me on ABC talking about *The Kite Runner*." What he didn't know was that ABC wasn't interested in his views on a movie. They were interested in talking about waterboarding, a subject that he knew little about. That didn't stop him from talking, however.

On national TV, he declared that waterboarding was "torture"—but that it was sadly necessary and effective, since Abu Zubaydah required only a single thirty- to thirty-five-second session, "and from that day on he answered [our] every question." In the coming days, this former Agency officer was interviewed on countless television programs, appeared in many print media stories, and obtained a paid consulting contract with ABC News.

About a year and a half later, a declassified CIA IG report was released showing that (at least in the mind of the IG) Abu Zubaydah had been waterboarded eighty-three times, not the one time the kite-flying former officer described. While the IG was wrong, too, their report demonstrated that the former Agency officer was not a good source. So how did he handle that disclosure? By saying that he heard the reports of the single waterboarding around the water cooler at CIA HQ and implying that the Agency had put out false information in the hallways, knowing that years later some of our employees would leak it, thereby misleading the American public. He told reporters, "In retrospect, it was a valuable lesson in how the CIA uses the fine arts of deception even among its own." His reward for his less-than-believable account? A book deal and a job as a U.S. Senate investigator.

One final story about these great pretenders. In the spring of 2011, I got word that news organizations were calling around regarding doing stories about a soon-to-be-published book by a former CIA officer who said he had been deeply involved in the interrogation program and was now calling it "torture." This officer, the media had been told, was a noted expert on counterterrorism. I had never heard of him. I spoke with a number of my former colleagues. They had never heard of him either. After considerable digging, we finally found someone who could confirm that at one time the guy had at least worked at the CIA. Turns out that he was stashed at Agency headquarters toward the end of a mediocre career while being investigated on several series of charges of wrongdoing and malfeasance. A requirement popped up for someone who spoke a particular language, and he was tapped for a short-term project. In his book, he lets readers leap to the conclusion that the man must be an expert in Arabic. In truth, it was one of the Romance languages. He was sent on a short assignment with specific instructions to have nothing to do with the actual interrogation of a prisoner then being held by a foreign intelligence service. His role was simply to be a go-between for the CIA and that intelligence service. That brief exposure, stretched beyond all credulity, turned into a book that sought to expose what he now says were the evil and unproductive CIA efforts to interrogate prisoners. While I have no desire to parse someone else's book, in my view, his would comfortably rest on the fiction shelves.

How can that happen? First, you should know that when the CIA's publication review board clears a book for publication, it does so on the basis of classification, not accuracy. Often when the publication review board demands that parts be cut ("redacted" is the term of art), readers think, "Oh, my gosh, there must be something really secret they are covering up here," when in fact it may be something quite routine.

I can tell you that it is much, much easier to get a book deal highly critical of the CIA than it is to write accurately and supportively of the work the Agency does. My caution is that the next time you read a news article or book or see a TV interview involving a former Agency officer telling you the secrets that "the CIA doesn't want you to know," give some thought to the possibility that he is making up stuff or leaping to conclusions that the media want to believe.

Readers may wonder why I don't give the names of the people I have just cited. There are a variety of reasons—but chief among them is my desire to write about actions rather than personalities. Those who closely follow the debate about the interrogation of al-Qa'ida detainees will easily be able to identify these people. My goal is simply to caution observers to take what they read from critics like this former FBI agent and two former CIA officers with a very large grain of salt.

Chapter 8

THE TAPES

It seemed like a good idea at the time. In April 2002, when a badly wounded Abu Zubaydah came into the CIA's custody, someone in CTC suggested that we videotape his interrogation. There were a couple of reasons why that seemed appropriate. Our people at the black site felt that tapes might help them study AZ's body language for nonverbal hints about the critical information he was trying to hide. Their view mirrored a famous quotation from Yogi Berra: "You can observe a lot by watching."

Those of us back at CIA headquarters, however, had a different motivation. Zubaydah had barely survived the bullet wounds suffered during his capture. He made it only because of the skill of a top-notch medical team, including that of a surgeon from Johns Hopkins whom the CIA flew out to treat him. But even with great medical care, AZ came close to dying on several occasions.

After a short period of recovery, he was judged well enough to be questioned during times of consciousness. But we were concerned that he might take a sudden turn for the worse. We wanted videotapes of the questioning sessions to be able to prove that nothing we did had worsened his condition, should he suddenly die.

So as AZ underwent his initial interrogation by CIA and FBI personnel in April, the tapes rolled. During this period, he occasionally gave up useful information but became increasingly resistant. There followed a few-week stretch during which he was essentially put in isolation, with very limited human contact. There was no reason to tape during that period.

Then, starting on August 4, 2002, AZ was reengaged and subjected to increasingly significant EITs, as described in an earlier chapter. During this period, Zubaydah was, once again, videotaped during his interrogation.

It turned out that the taping was of limited value as far as picking up nonverbal hints from his demeanor. We had enough eyeballs on him, both with him as he was interrogated and nearby watching live on closed-circuit TV, that our officers had no problem in picking up the significance of whatever he said or didn't say. It turned out that Agency personnel at the black site rarely turned to the videotape as they were preparing their intelligence reports to send back to Washington. Their contemporaneous notes and observations were detailed and accurate.

And the rationale for videotaping to demonstrate that "if he died it wasn't our fault" also melted away as AZ's medical condition stabilized and he grew stronger.

So at some point toward the end of the application of EITs to Abu Zubaydah, CIA officers at the black site asked themselves, "Why are we still taping?" They weren't getting anything out of the tapes, and since Agency officers could clearly be seen in the tapes interrogating AZ, it was clear that if the videos were ever released or leaked they could pose serious safety concerns for the people depicted on the tapes and their families.

When the EITs for Abu Zubaydah were in their final days, Agency officers at the black site sent word back to CIA headquarters that they viewed the continued retention of the videotapes as posing a serious counterintelligence and security risk and recommended that they be authorized to stop taping and destroy the tapes already on hand. There was no mention or concern that they were embarrassed by their own actions shown on the tapes. But they recognized that there was little to no intelligence value in making the tapes and it was clear that the images could put Agency officers at risk. So, as I recall, on

August 20, 2002, our people at the black site made a seemingly simple request that the tapes and taping be done away with. What followed was more than three years of hand-wringing and bureaucratic backpedaling until I made what turned out to be a fateful decision.

The request from the field to destroy the tapes went to our lawyers for consideration. The public, I suspect, would be very surprised to find out how ubiquitous lawyers are at the Agency. We had a ton of them. Don't get me wrong, I valued their counsel and support very much. We had a number of excellent lawyers assigned directly to CTC and many more throughout the Agency and on the staff of the general counsel. I am not sure exactly how many lawyers there were at the CIA but before 9/11, I believe they would have outnumbered the paramilitary officers we had in our Special Activities Division. General Mike Hayden, who was CIA director from May 2006 to February 2009, used to say that he had more lawyers on his staff than some of his foreign counterparts had officers.

The lawyers took the request to destroy the tapes under advisement. Meanwhile, the EIT program was just getting off the ground. When Congress came back from its annual summer recess in early September, I led a team from CTC to Capitol Hill to inform the senior leadership of our two oversight committees about the existence of the EIT program. Those discussions deserve special focus of their own, and I will get back to that—but for the tape story, suffice it to say that the congressional leadership was aware that the early interrogations had been videotaped but that we intended to stop that practice and destroy the existing tapes.

A little more than two months after the initial request from the field came in, the Agency's Office of General Counsel pronounced a decision on future taping. On October 25, headquarters told the field that in the future they should record one day's interrogation sessions on a videotape and then record the next day's on the same tape, recording over the previous material. That prevented the stockpile of videotapes from overwhelming the black site but did nothing to alleviate the concerns about all the tapes already made (by that time numbering more than ninety). By this time, a second high-value al-Qa'ida detainee, al-Nashiri, had joined AZ at the black site, and his interrogation was also videotaped.

A month later, in November 2002, headquarters advised the field that some news organizations were working hard to identify the location of the black site and that there might be press accounts soon speculating about where this secret site might be. That raised new security concerns, and the officers on scene sent in a renewed, expedited request for permission to destroy the existing stockpile of tapes. The lawyers said "no," or, more precisely, "not yet." They wouldn't sign off on the destruction of the tapes until they assured themselves that the written record of what happened in the interrogation sessions was accurate and complete. So they launched one of the assistant general counsels, a very senior Agency officer, out to the field, where he spent ten days viewing and cataloguing what he found to be ninety-two videotapes. On twelve of the tapes were scenes of EITs being applied. Many of the others were simply surveillance of our high-profile guests in their cells. The AGC diligently worked his way through the stack of tapes and reported that what he saw was in compliance with what the Department of Justice had authorized in August and was entirely consistent with what our officers in the field had reported back to headquarters in their written reports. Still, no decision was made to authorize the destruction of the tapes.

In December 2002, John Helgerson, the CIA inspector general (no fan of the EIT program), became aware of the existence of the tapes. The day after Christmas 2002, the Agency's general counsel informed the director of Central Intelligence that he had no objection "in principle" to CTC's continuing requests to destroy the tapes but recommended that we hold off until January, when a new Congress would be sworn in and fresh leadership would arrive at our oversight committees. The general counsel recommended that the CIA "inform" the committees of our intent, but also noted that if they objected and told us to retain the tapes or demanded to review them themselves, we would be in a strong position to deny the requests on security and operational grounds.

In meetings and conversations throughout the fall of 2002, I keep pushing for a decision that would allow us to do the right thing regarding the tapes. The delay was frustrating, but I had so many other things on my plate that I could not afford to obsess about the tapes. After all, we'd been waiting only four months, right?

In February 2003 the new leadership of the House and Senate intelligence committees was briefed on the existence of the tapes and the Agency's intent to destroy them. On February 4, Senator Pat Roberts (R-KS) quickly gave his assent. His Democratic counterpart, Senator Jay Rockefeller of West Virginia, was not present, but his staff director and another senior staffer were there and were expected to brief Rockefeller. The next day the chairman of the House committee, Porter Goss, and his ranking member, Congresswoman Jane Harman, were also briefed. Goss was supportive of our plan but Harman later sent a classified letter to the CIA urging us to "reconsider because even if the videotapes do not constitute an official record that must be preserved under the law, they could be the best proof that the written record is accurate."

Despite firm legal opinions from within the Agency that we

had the right to destroy the tapes and either support or luke-warm opposition from the Hill, the Agency's top leaders still wouldn't pull the trigger on destroying the tapes.

Then the IG did what the IG always does and decided to investigate. I had no problem with that. There had been some problems with the interrogation program—as with every program. Those issues were self-reported by our own people. More so than other organizations, the CIA regularly conducts due diligence on itself. This was to be an investigation of the entire interrogation program. That put a hold on any possible decision to take action about the tapes. Eventually, the IG staff concluded that destroying the tapes would be within our rights. Two investigators reviewed the tapes, logs, and cables at the foreign site and concluded that it was up to Agency man-agement to decide what to do with the tapes. I thought this was significant, since the IG shop had always been hostile to the EIT effort. Inspector General Helgerson once described it to a group of senior Agency officers as "that hideous program." If he couldn't find a reason to object to destroying the tapes, it had to be okay. But still, we waited.

In September another senior Agency attorney, a different assistant general counsel, took a crack at the legalities. After examining the issue, she reported in writing that the record showed that for "grave national security reasons," retention of the tapes presented "grave risk" to the personal safety of our officers and required the destruction of the tapes. And still, we waited.

In January 2004 the same attorney reiterated her written opinion but added that we should consult the inspector general (who had already weighed in on the matter) before taking ac-tion. And still, we waited.

Yet another assistant general counsel provided a written

opinion in early April saying that there were no legal requirements for the Agency to retain the tapes.

In late April 2004, there was an explosive event that added to our conviction that getting rid of the tapes was vitally important. That month, truly awful photographs appeared in the media showing U.S. Army troops brutally abusing Iraqis held at the Abu Ghraib prison. The disgraceful and disgusting treatment of these prisoners had absolutely nothing to do with the interrogation program run by the CIA. Our program, blessed by the highest legal authorities in the land, conducted by trained professionals, and applied to only a handful of the most important terrorists on the planet, bore no relation to the unauthorized actions of a handful of low-level army troops. The justifiable outcry about the abusive treatment shown in the Abu Ghraib photos, first on *60 Minutes II* and later in magazines and newspapers around the globe, did huge harm to the image of the United States. President Bush apologized for the actions of these sick soldiers and Secretary of Defense Rumsfeld offered his resignation to atone for their mindless actions.

We knew that if the photos of CIA officers conducting authorized EITs ever got out, the difference between a legal, authorized, necessary, and safe program and the mindless actions of some MPs would be buried by the impact of the images. The propaganda damage to the image of America would be immense. But my main concern then, and always, was for the safety of my officers.

The image of Private Lynndie England holding a leash attached to a naked, anonymous Iraqi was devastating. The reaction from around the world was one of disgust. She was later (quite appropriately) sentenced to three years in prison and dishonorably discharged. But what if a photo of a senior al-Qa'ida leader being waterboarded by CIA officers were to get out? The image might be disturbing, but more troubling to me would be the possibility that al-Qa'ida and its supporters would use the photo to track down Agency officers and exact revenge on them or their families. To me the Abu Ghraib debacle provided more evidence that it was urgent to take action about the CIA videotapes. To others it was yet another reason to do nothing.

By this time, the bureaucratic "mother-may-I?" instincts of the CIA had kicked into high gear. The Agency's general counsel, Scott Muller, decided to check with senior lawyers at the Department of Justice and the Office of the Vice President for their views. Not unexpectedly, the answer he got was that it probably wasn't a good idea to destroy the tapes "right now." And so, we waited.

The CIA IG completed the lengthy (and in my view highly flawed) report on the Agency's overall interrogation program in May. That report was forwarded to the leadership of the House and Senate intelligence committees in June. The report contained three substantive paragraphs about the videotaping of interrogations.

We know some people on the Hill read the report. Senator Rockefeller, who would later claim that he and the committee were kept largely in the dark about the issue, requested several documents mentioned in the IG report, including the document created by the assistant general counsel who had reviewed and inventoried the tapes for the express purpose of determining whether it was okay for us to destroy them.

Frequently during the several-year period after our officers in the field first requested permission to destroy the tapes, I would bring up to the general counsel and other senior Agency officials my concerns about the lack of a decision and the foot-dragging that we were experiencing. To bureaucrats in Washington, discussions over the fate of the videos were an interesting legalistic debate. To the men and women depicted on the tapes, the lack of will to remove this potential threat to their personal safety was more than a little troubling. By this time I had moved up to become the deputy director of Operations. I was now one of "them," one of the "seventh-floor" people who were supposed to make all the big decisions. I remained something of a pest to the Office of the General Counsel, trying to get a decision, and the right one, made.

I later learned that in March of 2005 the acting general counsel, John Rizzo, a highly experienced and capable career Agency lawyer (known for his seemingly never-ending supply of tailored suits with matching suspenders, socks, and pocket squares), had met with CIA director Porter Goss and told him of the great angst within CTC and the Directorate of Operations about this issue, which at that point had lingered more than two and a half years since it had first been raised. Goss, like his predecessor, was reportedly uncomfortable about ordering the elimination of the tapes. Rizzo decided to raise the issue again with the White House counsel, Harriet Miers. At the time, Miers was on the brink of being nominated as a Supreme Court justice, a nomination that would be withdrawn a few months after it was made. She apparently told Rizzo that she, too, was uncomfortable with our ridding ourselves of the tape albatross just then. I say "apparently," because I have no recollection of Rizzo ever sharing with me her views, except for being told orally that she had "not yet" given her okay. Years later, the special prosecutor who would be appointed to look into the matter surfaced a single email Rizzo allegedly sent me in 2005 saying Miers had expressed qualms, but if I ever saw it (and I don't think I did), it made no impact on me. Just another lawyer saying: "I'd rather you not. . . ."

In July there were meetings at the White House during which Rizzo and other CIA lawyers met with Miers and reps from the NSC and the vice president's staff. The consensus,

I later learned, was that while there was no—repeat, no—requirement to retain the tapes, they recommended that the newly created director of national intelligence and the Office of the Attorney General be "briefed" before the destruction took place.

The DNI, Ambassador John Negroponte, reportedly told Goss that he opposed the destruction of the tapes despite the assessment that there was no legal constraint from doing so. My successor as chief of CTC told Negroponte that continued retention of the tapes would be quite distressing to our employees who were depicted on them and could place them and their families at risk. In any case, Negroponte's objections were never conveyed to me as an "order," just an "opinion."

The seemingly endless debate stretched on into the fall, now more than three years after it had started. At one point some lawyers suggested transferring the tapes from the field, where they had always been, back to headquarters. Fortunately, that idea was dropped. Bringing them back to Washington would only ensure that the tapes would be copied, passed around, widely discussed, and most likely result in a decision on someone's part to officially release or to leak them.

To say I was getting frustrated would be a massive understatement. My chief of staff held a meeting with CTC lawyers and other parties and asked two questions: (1) Is the destruction of the tapes legal? and (2) Did I, as director of the National Clandestine Service, have the authority to make that decision on my own? The answer she got to both questions was: Yes.

As must be abundantly clear by now, nothing is that easy in Washington. In order to do what the field had asked us to do thirty-eight months before, we had to require them to ask us again. To make sure we got the right question, so that we could give the right answer, on November 4, 2005, lawyers in CTC (we had our own lawyers who were separate from the larger contingent in the General Counsel's Office) drafted a cable that could be sent to the field with instructions that they cut and paste the appropriate language from the cable and put it into their own cable back to us. The instructions basically were: "Ask us in this way and we will say yes." The draft language was sent to the Office of the General Counsel for coordination at the same time it was sent to the field.

The next day, a Saturday, the field dutifully sent a cable to headquarters asking for permission to destroy the tapes. The language was just right, of course, since our lawyers had drafted it. I asked my chief of staff to prepare a cable granting permission. On most matters I would just instruct my staff on what action to take and let them handle the administrative details. But this had been such an ordeal that I wanted to personally handle what I thought was the end of a long bureaucratic nightmare.

In fact it was just the beginning. My chief of staff drafted a cable approving the action that we had been trying to accomplish for so long. The cable left nothing to chance. It even told them *how* to get rid of the tapes. They were to use an industrial-strength shredder to do the deed. On Tuesday, November 8, after scrutinizing the cable on my computer for a while, I thought about the decision. I was not depriving anyone of information about what was done or what was said, I was just getting rid of some ugly visuals that could put the lives of my people at risk. I took a deep breath of weary satisfaction and hit Send.

The next day, November 9, the field sent in a cable reporting that the shredder had done its work. The machine, the likes of which have been in use at U.S. government facilities for more than thirty-five years, can chew through hundreds of pounds of material in a single hour. The device's five spinning and two stationary steel blades are designed to chop up DVDs,

CDs, cell phones, credit cards, X-rays, and other optical media and produce tiny, unrecognizable bits that are vacuumed out into giant, heavy-duty, plastic trash bags. Our problem had been reduced to confetti—or so we thought.

Apparently we had gotten ahead of ourselves. We had asked the Office of General Counsel to approve the language we sent to the field providing the wording they sent back to us asking permission to destroy the tapes. The day after the tapes were destroyed, the General Counsel's Office got around to telling us that our language was okay. "That's good to hear," CTC officials told them, "because Jose directed the field to destroy the tapes pursuant to their request and they did . . . yesterday."

Although he didn't confront me, Rizzo reportedly was not a happy camper. He told my chief of staff that he thought that the plan was that when the field made their request (again), he would have a chance to review it (again) and take it to Goss for discussion (again). That wasn't my understanding and I wasn't going to sit around another three years waiting for people to get up the courage to make a decision that I had been told I could legally make on my own.

Rizzo reportedly informed Harriet Miers at the White House that I had preempted the system's ability to dither about the decision further. At the time, I did not directly hear anything about my actions from the White House. Five years later, I had an opportunity to discuss the matter with a very senior former member of the Bush White House. I don't have permission to quote him by name but he confirmed my suspicions. He said that when senior White House and NSC officials heard about my action, there was a collective sigh of relief. He conveyed to me that they were delighted with what I had done. Just as significantly, he confirmed my belief that if I had waited for them to give me the go-ahead, I would still be waiting.

I recall only one conversation about this matter with CIA

director Goss after my order to destroy the tapes. He was calm and gentlemanly as always. I told him that if this later became a big issue, I was willing to take the heat for it. He bemusedly speculated that if it did, *he* would be the one taking the heat.

Years later I heard that Goss felt that I had denied him the opportunity to find a solution to the tape problem. But I was convinced, then and now, that the matter would have lingered on without resolution if I had not acted. In any case, Goss has told people that he believes I was well within my rights to make the decision I did. It was also years later when I learned that there were questions about whether the tapes were relevant to requests for documents in legal proceedings that were ongoing at the time. But it was my view that if the lawyers told me it was okay to destroy the tapes, I was on solid ground.

After my single discussion with Goss in August 2005 about my decision to order the tapes destroyed, things got quiet. I had nothing to worry about. Nothing, other than a continuing war on terror, the situation in Iraq, which was spiraling out of control, and the regular series of threats that the chief of the clandestine service has to deal with, and the rest of the world, or so I thought.

One thing that did not get done, or perhaps did not get done well enough, was notifying our congressional overseers that the tapes had finally been destroyed. Frankly, I did not give that a thought. I didn't view telling Congress as my responsibility. Someone, perhaps the Office of General Counsel or the Office of Congressional Affairs, should have quickly informed the committee leadership. I didn't think of it and apparently neither did anyone else. Had we done so, it might have mitigated some problems down the road. On the other hand, the cynic in me says that it also might have just accelerated the leaking of the whole issue to the press.

Time and the Agency marched on. By May 2006 the CIA

had another new director, the tenth and final one for whom I would work. General Mike Hayden, former head of the National Security Agency and most recently top deputy to the DNI, John Negroponte, had been selected to succeed Porter Goss. Because the EIT program was increasingly drawing public scrutiny and criticism, one of his early decisions was to take the May 2004 IG report on the interrogation program and share it with the entire oversight committees and their staffs (previously only the committee leadership had had access to it). Despite the fact that Hayden, like his predecessors and those of us in the Directorate of Operations, thought the report was wrong in many respects, he wanted to set the tone of inclusiveness by sharing it with the broad swath of our overseers. Recall, now, that the report had three lengthy paragraphs on the past use of videotapes.

In August 2006, Hayden sent a four-page memo to the national security advisor, Steve Hadley, saying that in his opinion it was time to bring the CIA's detention program out of the shadows. We were never set up to be jailers, and he explained that because of changes in the law, leaks in the media, and diminishing returns from the senior al-Qa'ida operatives in our custody, he believed that the time was ripe to move the most senior detainees to Guantanamo Bay, empty the black sites, and reveal the broad outline of what had been done in them.

On September 6, 2006, President Bush announced that Abu Zubaydah, KSM, and twelve other top al-Qa'ida operatives had been moved to Gitmo. He publicly confirmed, for the first time, some of the details of the interrogation program that we firmly believed was not just the CIA's program, not the Bush administration's program, but America's.

In March and April 2007, Agency lawyers went to SCIFs (Secure Compartmented Information Facilities) on Capitol Hill, where a large number of Hill staffers were briefed in much greater detail about the EIT program. In Agency parlance they were brought into the "compartment." At least fifteen Senate staffers and a number of House staffers were given deep insight into the program, including the fact that tapes had once existed and had since been destroyed. In routine (although classified) communication with the Hill through that spring, Hayden told some members of Congress that the tapes had proven of no use for intelligence purposes and that the practice of making them had ended and existing tapes had been destroyed.

During this period, a cottage industry had arisen of journalists and authors trying to unearth juicy details about the interrogation program. They played games of "can you top this" and fought over anonymous sources who would reveal the latest sordid details about these still-secret activities.

Mike Hayden remembers exactly where he was when he heard that word of the destruction of the tapes had leaked. It was November 15, 2007, and he was sitting at Andrews Air Force Base waiting for a massive storm to lift so that he could fly to New York City and receive an award from a group called the Business Executives for National Security. While he was waiting in the distinguished visitor lounge, a member of his staff got a call from headquarters. A former intelligence official had called the office to let the Agency know that Mark Mazzetti, a reporter for the *New York Times,* was calling around Capitol Hill and to former Agency officials asking about the destruction of videotapes. From the sound of it, Mazzetti had quite a lot of information and was putting the worst possible spin on the decision.

There is no savvier Washington insider than Mike Hayden, and you didn't have to paint a picture for him. Take a story about the destruction of secret videotapes containing images of enhanced interrogation at black sites, sprinkle in a liberal dose of such phrases as "obstruction of justice," and you have a made-for-D.C. scandal. The storm never cleared for Hayden. His trip to New York was canceled. And it took more than three years for the storm to clear for me.

Since he was not director when the tapes were made or when they were destroyed, the first thing Hayden had to do was some fact-finding. He was vaguely familiar with the tapes issue when he was deputy DNI. While he knew a little about the matter, it has not been a front-burner issue for him. Now it was. Hayden directed his senior staff to call together representatives from the Directorate of Operations and the General Counsel's Office, as well as representatives from Legislative Affairs, the IG's Office, and the public affairs staff to come together and reconstruct what had happened and why. Because the issue had been so highly classified and tightly compartmented, that wasn't easy to do. The people in the press office braced themselves for what they expected to be an early call from the *New York Times* asking questions about the tapes.

I wasn't on hand to be of much help when the initial tipoffs about the press interest came in. In September, I had concluded that I was burned out. After thirty-one years at the Agency I was out of gas. It was time to step aside and let someone else lead the clandestine service. When he became CIA director, Hayden had persuaded Steve Kappes (the former DDO who left the Agency rather than cave to the demands of the Gosslings) to return to be his deputy. When I decided to retire, Kappes convinced his former deputy, Mike Sulick (the guy whose dustup with Goss's chief of staff precipitated their joint departure), to return as well and take over my job. It was a remarkable change of fortune since two years before.

The CIA has a valuable and necessary "transition" program that allows retiring officers to both wrap up their government careers and learn, often after decades of living undercover, how to come out of the cold and into the sunlight. It is not an easy thing to write a résumé when most of what you have done for the past three decades is still considered secret. Nor is it easy to explain how your skills running agents and stealing secrets might be of benefit to a future civilian employer. So I was immersed in the transition process, with the intent to retire at the first of the year.

I was taking a few days off from this transition process to take one of my sons back to college in Georgia when I got a frantic call from my usually unflappable former chief of staff. She told me about the *New York Times'* efforts to expose the tape-destruction effort and the impression that my actions would be painted in the worst possible light. I wasn't too concerned. I knew what I had done was right and that there was a lengthy paper trail to demonstrate that we hadn't acted without considerable prior thought and consultation. How bad could this be? I asked myself.

The CIA's public affairs shop waited for the call from the *New York Times* the rest of that week in mid-November. They waited the next week, Thanksgiving week, and the week after that. No questions came about the tape issue. Mazzetti was one of the best reporters who routinely covered intelligence, and he was in regular contact about other matters, but said nothing about the tapes. It was getting frustrating waiting for the expected shoe to drop.

Although I was in the transition program, I hadn't quite shed myself of all my official duties. A group of House intelligence committee members and staffers had scheduled an official trip to Latin America, and because I was so well-known, both to them and to the countries they were visiting, they asked me to go along as a semi-official escort. These kinds of trips are generally a mixture of official briefings, meetings with host country officials and intelligence service reps, and occasional events to give the congressional delegation a taste of the local culture.

We were at one such event in Buenos Aries, where colorfully dressed locals were dancing the tango on Calle La Florida, when the committee's majority chief counsel, Jeremy Bash, asked me, "What is this I hear about an issue involving the Agency destroying some videotapes?" Rather than tell the story multiple times, I called all the members and other staffers together, right there in the street, and gave a brief synopsis of what was done and why. It shouldn't have been new business for any of them. I believed they all had been briefed on the existence of the tapes and their destruction before, but I tried to quickly put the story in context for them. There wasn't much reaction from most of those present—perhaps they wanted to get back to tango-watching—but I distinctly remember Bash telling me: "Jose, you were justified in what you did."

The long-awaited call from the *New York Times* finally came to CIA public affairs in the early evening of Wednesday, December 5. The reporter indicated that he had a lot of information, confirmed by various current and former government officials, and that his paper was prepared to publish the story in the next few days. Since we knew that he had been working on the story for at least the better part of a month, the call left the impression that he was going through the motions of soliciting the official response to go along with a story that had already largely been written.

One of the great frustrations of people who work at places like the CIA is the fact that too often they hear bad news about their own organization first by reading it in the newspaper. Hayden was determined not to let that be the case in this instance. The team that he had tasked with looking into the matter on November 16 had a pretty good handle on the issue and quickly drafted a statement that he could share with the Agency workforce.

The statement started by saying, "The press has learned that back in 2002, during the initial stage of our terrorist detention program, CIA videotaped interrogations, and destroyed the tapes in 2005." While Hayden made clear that while the actions took place long before he became director of the CIA, he did not take the easy way out and hide behind an "it didn't happen on my watch" excuse. He told the workforce that "the decision to destroy the tapes was made within CIA itself," adding that the decision was made "in line with the law." He reported that leaders of the Agency's oversight committees had been "informed of the videos years ago and of the Agency's intention to dispose of the material." Hayden stressed that the interrogation program was "of great value to our country. It has helped disrupt terrorist operations and saved lives." He predicted, however, that "we may see misinterpretation of the facts in the days ahead." A CIA director has never been more right.

Hayden directed that the statement be released to CIA employees worldwide. At about the same time it was delivered to the *New York Times*. As might be expected, an unclassified statement on such an explosive matter leaked almost instantly. A reporter from the Associated Press called and was given the same statement. The *New York Times* rushed its story onto its website in an effort to protect its "scoop." The AP, as wire services typically do, played the matter straight, citing Hayden's explanation for why the tapes were destroyed: "Out of fear that they would leak to the public and compromise the identities of U.S. questioners." The *New York Times,* on the other hand, relied on the spin from unnamed current and former government officials saying that the "tapes were destroyed in part because officers were concerned that video showing harsh inter-rogation methods could expose agency officials to legal risks." That was never the case.

There was one other interesting difference between the first AP story on the destruction of the tapes and that of the *New York Times*. The AP portrayed the action, as Hayden had, as a decision of the Agency. The *Times* quoted "current and former intelligence officials" as saying that the decision was made by "Jose A. Rodriguez, Jr." Well, at least they got that part right.

Over the years casual observers would have been forgiven if they assumed the "C" in "CIA" stood for "controversial." The Agency has found itself embroiled in scandal and controversy on a regular basis. But even veteran Agency watchers were stunned at the response to the initial reports about the destruc-tion of the tapes. It was the lead story in newspapers around the world, the top item on television newscasts, and finger-pointing fodder for politicians and pundits everywhere.

I cannot adequately explain how much of a shock it is for someone like me, who had spent the past thirty-one years living undercover, to turn on the network nightly news pro-grams and see my official government photo (which had been considered classified until a few months before) flashed on the screen as the alleged perpetrator of some purported dastardly deed.

Just three months before, as I was preparing to retire, I had gone through the process at the Agency of dropping my cover. One reason I did so was to allow me to participate in a border security conference in El Paso, Texas, at the invitation of Con-gressman Silvestre Reyes, chairman of the House Permanent Select Committee on Intelligence. My main motivation for coming out of the shadows was so that I could speak out on behalf of minority recruitment in the intelligence service. I wanted young men and women to see that not only is it possible for people of diverse heritages to rise to the top of the clandestine service, but in many ways being a member of a minority can give you an operational advantage. The CIA, and all of government, had done a lousy job of bringing minorities into its ranks and I hoped to make some progress in addressing that shortfall in my final months as an Agency employee. Still, standing up in front of four hundred people in a public setting, with TV cameras rolling, and saying, "My name is Jose Rodriguez; I'm the director of the National Clandestine Service, the espionage service of the United States of America" ran counter to everything I had done for the past three decades. I told people at the time that lifting your cover was like "dropping trou in public." Not a comfortable feeling.

Congressman Reyes introduced me at the conference. With more than a little hyperbole, he favorably compared my past exploits to those of Jack Bauer on the TV show *24*. He called me "an American hero." Those were the last kind words I would hear from a member of Congress for quite some time.

When something like the tape-destruction story breaks in the media, reporters go to the old reliable quote machines who are always ready with an opinion whether they have the facts or not. In the case of this story, they didn't disappoint. In the first twenty-four hours after the allegations surfaced, Senator Ted Kennedy (D-MA) declared, "We haven't seen anything like this since the eighteen-and-a-half-minute gap in the tapes of President Richard Nixon." On the floor of the Senate he asked, "What would cause the CIA to take this action?" And he responded to his own question: "The answer is obvious—cover up." Senate Armed Services chairman Carl Levin (D-MI) declared that General Hayden's explanation of the tape destruction was "a pathetic excuse."

As luck would have it, the very day that the tapes story first appeared in the nation's newspapers, Friday, December 7 (the anniversary of Pearl Harbor), was also the day of the CIA's annual holiday party. It is scheduled months in advance, and the Agency's director typically invites senior government officials, members of Congress, former CIA directors, and top Agency officers (who are not undercover) to a festive occasion held in the main lobby of the headquarters. The reception area is adorned with poinsettias, a small combo plays holiday music, and guests chow down on heavy hors d'oeuvres prepared by Agency chefs, some of whom trained at the *other* CIA, the Culinary Institute of America. Hayden was late for his own party, however, detained in his office seven floors above with urgent phone calls from the White House, the attorney general, and others trying to get a handle on the crisis. Some of the congressional invitees arrived fresh from media appearances at which they bashed the Agency handling of the tapes matter. Journalists in attendance worked the crowd at the off-the-record party for fresh insights into the burgeoning scandal. Mark Mazzetti of the *New York Times,* who had been the first reporter to pursue the story, had been on the invitation list, but did not attend.

Since Washington is the kind of place it is, it was only a short time after the first stories broke before people all over town started to distance themselves from my controversial decision. ABC News reported on the evening of December 7 that "according to three officials," White House counsel Harriet Miers had "urged the CIA not to destroy the tapes." The next day the *New York Times* had two front-page stories about the matter. The lead of a story, by Mark Mazzetti, that morning had said that "White House and Justice Department officials, along with senior members of Congress, advised the Central Intelligence Agency in 2003 against a plan to destroy hundreds of hours of videotapes," citing "government officials" as the source. Mazzetti added that the CIA's "own top lawyer, John A. Rizzo," was "angry at the decision." Mazzetti wrote that I had "reversed" a previous decision to preserve the tapes, which was simply untrue. No one had made any decision for three years until I did what needed to be done. The AP quoted "a former intelligence official" as saying that then–CIA director Porter Goss was "upset with the tapes' destruction," adding, however, that "though Goss believed this was a bad judgment it falls within the prerogative of the directorate of operations."

Armchair critics weighed in, too. Law professors were quick to pronounce the tapes' destruction a "very big deal" and possible "obstruction of justice." I didn't need my law school diploma to know that seeing your name in the same sentence as the words "obstruction of justice" is not a good thing. I called one of the senior lawyers in the Directorate of Operations and said: "I need a good private attorney who could obtain security clearances. Can you recommend someone?" It was clear that my interests and those perceived by the CIA might not be identical anymore. He promised to get back to me.

As soon as the media firestorm ignited, news organizations tried to track me down to get a comment or, at a minimum, get a picture of me refusing to comment. Despite the fact that I had until recently been undercover, and despite the fact that at the time there were more than five hundred Jose A. Rodriguezes in Virginia, Maryland, and the District of Columbia, all places where CIA headquarters employees typically live, within a few hours there were camera crews knocking at the door of my home, slipping notes and business cards under the door, and pestering my neighbors. The notes generally said that they simply wanted to offer me a chance to respond to "what everyone else was saying" about me. The reporters didn't go so far as to specify what that might be. When we didn't answer the doorbell, one news crew drove fifty feet up the street and just parked, staring at the house for hours on end.

Since the first stories on the tape controversy had run on Thursday, December 6, and the crescendo built on Friday, I figured things would calm down a little over the weekend. Wrong again. On December 8, the Justice Department and CIA inspector general issued a rare Saturday press release. In an effort to manage the crisis, they announced that they were launching a joint preliminary inquiry into the tapes' destruction to determine if a full-fledged investigation and potential criminal charges were called for. The *Los Angeles Times* quoted an unnamed senior U.S. official as saying, "Everybody from the top on down told them not to do it, and still they went ahead and did it anyway." I was starting to feel a little lonely.

Wasting little time, the next week congressional oversight committees called Director Hayden to testify for six hours over two days. Although they were closed sessions, the members wasted no time running out to the "stake out" positions outside the hearing rooms to tell the waiting media that they were not satisfied and would demand more.

Despite feeling literally and figuratively under siege, I couldn't sit still. My parents' sixtieth wedding anniversary was coming up, and Patti and I and the boys were scheduled to fly to Puerto Rico for the festivities. I called CIA director Hayden to thank him for his support and to tell him where I was going. I didn't want him to hear that the media followed me to the airport and speculate that I was making a run for the border. Hayden was cool, calm, and supportive, as he was throughout the ordeal. But I suspect he, too, was surprised at the vehemence of some of the reporting on the tapes issue. Some news accounts even began referring to the matter as "Tapes-gate." Fortunately that label didn't stick.

We landed in San Juan, rented a car, and made the

three-hour drive across the island to my parents' home in Mayaguez. While en route to my parents' I got a cell phone call from an Agency attorney, who told me that the renowned criminal defense attorney Bob Bennett had agreed to help me and that I should call him as soon as possible. I agreed to do so.

After arriving and spending a little time trying to explain to my elderly parents why I was in such hot water, I excused myself to use my mother's antiquated computer to log on to the internet and see how the news coverage was going.

Coño! I thought. I knew I might someday take a little heat over this, but I was starting to feel like Joan of Arc. I decided to call Bob Bennett. Hearing that an attorney like Bennett is willing to help you is like hearing that the pope is waiting to bless you. Bennett is a legendary Washington lawyer who represented President Clinton during the Lewinsky scandal and Caspar Weinberger during Iran-Contra. It was only later that I wondered if the Agency thought I needed a world-class defender because I was in a world of trouble.

While my siblings and family friends were celebrating my parents' anniversary, I excused myself again to make a call to Bennett. Over the next week, I spoke to him for hours, giving him as much information as I could share over the phone. He asked me to lay out the whole story as best I could remember it. When I finished my tale he simply said, "Okay. Come see me when you get back to town."

I felt awful about my notoriety intruding on what was supposed to be a festive occasion for my parents. Just a few months before, my cover had been lifted, and for the first time in thirty years they could tell their friends and neighbors what their son really did for a living. For a few short months they could tell friends that a member of Congress had called their son a hero. Now everyone could read stories in which lots of senators and other top officials called him a bum.

When we returned to Washington, my parents came with us. I tried to project great confidence that this was a tempest in a teapot. "It'll all blow over before you know it," I told Patti, my parents, my siblings, and the boys. I could tell they weren't buying the happy-face I was painting on the situation. But having the whole family together was a source of great strength for me.

Once back in the D.C. area, I went downtown to meet Bob Bennett and his longtime law partner Carl Rauh in person. I laid out the story in even greater detail as he silently took notes. Bob had been at the center of scores of high-profile legal battles. He would know how much trouble I was in. When I finished, he put down his pen. "I've got it," he said as he closed his notebook. What he said next gave me great comfort. "You are a hero," he simply said.

There weren't a lot of people in Congress who appeared to agree with Bennett. The announcement of a preliminary joint DOJ-CIA inspector general investigation didn't seem to slow the crowd with pitchforks and torches demanding that more formal proceedings begin right away. Senator Joe Biden (D-DE), who was running for his party's presidential nomination at the time, was among those who called for an "independent counsel," saying that the administration didn't have "the credibility to do it on their own."

But the congressional intelligence oversight committees weren't about to miss a chance to be center stage in a media frenzy like this. Both the Senate committee, chaired by Senator Rockefeller, and the House committee, chaired by Congressman Reyes, announced plans to hold hearings to get to the bottom of the matter and to call this Rodriguez fellow who caused all this trouble as a witness. "Not so fast," the Department of Justice said. DOJ officials feared that Congress would screw up their criminal investigation. Bob Bennett told reporters that he was not going to let his client "be a piñata for people with a political agenda during an election year." Whether it was intentional or not, I enjoyed the allusion to my Hispanic heritage.

One of the things that got congressional members riled up was the implication in Hayden's original press statement that "our oversight committees also have been told that the videos were, in fact, destroyed." While this was true, many of the members weren't personally informed until well after the tapes were destroyed, and the implication that they might have known and remained silent about an action they now were condemning really fired them up.

The anger was bipartisan. Republican congressman Pete Hoekstra said on *Fox News Sunday* that "certain statements that came out of the [intelligence] community might have been misleading." He went on to rant about an intelligence community that "is incompetent, is arrogant, and it has developed—it's become political." His take throughout the tapes matter was that the CIA didn't believe it was "accountable to the president" or "accountable to Congress." He had made his conclusions before any hearings were held. Democratic congresswoman Jane Harman piled on, too, saying that our actions smelled "like a cover-up of the cover-up."

Hoeskstra said the House committee would likely defy any suggestion by DOJ that they delay their hearings until Justice's investigation could take place. He predicted that the committee would issue subpoenas for witnesses and documents but had not decided if it would offer immunity in exchange for any testimony.

The Agency and General Hayden were in quite a fix. They relied on the oversight committees to authorize and fund the CIA's activities and couldn't afford to alienate them too severely.

On the other hand, when DOJ is urging you not to do something for fear of impeding a criminal investigation, you need to pay attention.

Meanwhile, the media response continued to build. Scores of newspapers around the country editorialized about the tapes matter. I never saw a single one that was in any way supportive of the action I had ordered. Of course, the editorial writers had precious little information on which to base their views, but it seemed information was not a requirement before rushing to judgment.

January 2, 2008, was memorable for a couple of reasons. After thirty-one years as a CIA officer, it was my next-to-last day as an Agency employee. Rather than having a grand retirement ceremony in the CIA headquarters, as I might have envisioned, I drove to a nondescript outlying Agency building in the northern Virginia suburbs, where I unceremoniously handed my access badge that had opened doors around the world to a security guard and walked to my car by myself. I drove home to a very uncertain future.

That same day, Attorney General Michael Mukasey announced the launching of a full-blown criminal investigation into the destruction of the tapes. The recently confirmed Mukasey also revealed that he had assigned a dogged veteran career prosecutor, John H. Durham, as a special prosecutor, reporting directly to the deputy attorney general.

I understood why Mukasey felt he had to do what he did. The heat was too intense for him to declare "no harm, no foul." Still, it was not a good feeling to read in his announcement the statement that there was "sufficient predication to warrant a criminal investigation of a potential felony."

I was relieved that at least he had not succumbed to the pressure to appoint an independent counsel, who would have reported to no one. History had shown that independent counsels tended to go on forever, dragging out investigations interminably and becoming what some people in Washington call "a self-licking ice cream cone," in other words, an organization that serves no useful purpose other than to perpetuate its own existence. Knowing that the record was replete with documentation that various lawyers had told me in writing that I was empowered to do what I did, I figured the investigation might last a couple of months before it was dismissed. That turned out to be not one of my more accurate intelligence predictions.

Suddenly I found myself retired, under criminal investigation, and (except for my family) feeling pretty much alone. Don't get me wrong. I got a lot of calls of support from friends and former colleagues, but I likened it to a funeral. Lots of people show up for the service and express their sympathies, but then they go home or back to work and get on with their lives. Only the next of kin are left to deal with their sense of enormous loss.

During the late fall, when I was in the transition program, I was looking forward to getting a civilian job and starting a new phase of my life. Senior operations officers from the CIA have a pretty good track record of landing challenging and well-paid jobs in the private sector when they leave the clandestine service. I had had several flattering inquiries about my availability and had even traveled to New York City a couple of times to discuss some intriguing job prospects. Needless to say, having the attorney general announce that you are under criminal investigation does not give a boost to your employment prospects. Potential employers suddenly became vague, distant, and noncommittal. As time passed, I began to wonder, even if someone did offer me a job, could I in good faith accept it knowing that at any moment I might have to drop everything to focus on my own defense?

Eventually a standoff between the congressional oversight committees and the Department of Justice was resolved so that they could continue their hearings. The House committee scheduled a hearing for January 16 and wanted to call both John Rizzo and me to testify. Rizzo agreed to meet with the panel.

Bob Bennett told me that many people who consider themselves completely innocent, as I did, are offended at the notion of declining to testify and exercising their Fifth Amendment rights. He gingerly approached the subject with me. "Jose, you and I know that you have done nothing wrong, but it is my legal advice that you go before the committee only if they subpoena you and, if they do, take the Fifth unless they grant you immunity in exchange for your testimony." From his tone I think he was expecting me to fight him on it.

"Absolutely!" I said. "I've been reading the shit these members of Congress have been saying about me. They've already convicted me. I'd be crazy to talk to them while DOJ is looking for some discrepancy to hang me on." Bennett gave me a satisfied smile.

Word started getting out that I was not planning on volunteering to be a piñata for the committee, and they weren't happy. Congressman Hoekstra told reporters, "We need to get Jose Rodriguez in here to testify. Jose was responsible for this— or it appears that most press reports and other reports indicate that Jose was responsible for this decision to destroy the tapes." ABC News quoted Alan Baron, a former U.S. prosecutor, as saying, "If (Rodriguez) takes the Fifth Amendment, if there is a hearing, it's like putting on *Hamlet* without the prince."

Bob Bennett held his ground and the committee relented, deciding not to call me. They tried to save face by announcing that they reserved the right to call me at a later date. Left unsaid was that I reserved the right to tell them to go pound sand.

Rizzo showed up as scheduled on January 16. Again, it was a closed session, although members and staffers felt free to characterize it to the press. The *Washington Post* quoted Hoekstra as saying, "It appears from what we have seen to date that Rodriguez may not have been following instructions" when he ordered the tapes destroyed. An anonymous source told the *Post,* "It smells like a cover-up, but the question is whether it was illegal or not." The *New York Times* quoted Hoekstra as saying, "Matter of fact, it appears that [Rodriguez] got direction to make sure the tapes were not destroyed." Bob Bennett was obliged to respond to that charge, saying: "Nobody, to our knowledge, ever instructed him not to destroy the tapes."

As is typical when CIA officials testify before Congress, Rizzo showed up with a supporting cast of characters from the Office of Congressional Affairs and other agency officials. These "back benchers" are common at almost all hearings. But this time the committee took offense and reportedly asked those people who they were and why they were present. Not satisfied with the answer, the committee ejected them all from the session, leaving only Rizzo. Some of the members went to the media stakeout area after the hearing to declare me guilty, but no one was there to provide an alternative point of view. All Rizzo was able to say to the press after the hearing was: "I told the truth."

For over a month, the tale of the tapes had been a big deal. It was the subject of countless news stories, Op-Eds, editorials, and hearings, and of idle speculation. And then things got quiet. Very quiet.

There were no new leaks and fewer new pronouncements of my guilt from members of Congress, and Washington appeared to move on to other matters. There was a presidential election coming up in the fall, and the focus on this one "scandal" had well exceeded the typical life span of a D.C. crisis.

It was quiet but I knew that the special prosecutor, John Durham, and his staff were hard at work in the background. But I was disconnected from all of it. I was sitting at home waiting for someone to declare me innocent, yet knowing that at any moment I could hear that I was about to be indicted. During my time at the Agency I had known more than a handful of fine officers who were indicted for things they did not do—or for things they did that should never have been judged illegal. So the knowledge that everything I had done was done for good and honorable reasons was only of partial comfort.

I continued my job search, but potential employers were staying away from me as if I had a communicable disease. A number of former Agency friends tried to be helpful, giving me advice and sharing contacts in an effort to find some employer, any employer, who might take a chance on someone like me with a cloud hanging over his head. The search was fruitless. Eventually I set up my own consulting firm. Some courageous outfits were willing to take my advice on a piecemeal basis. That seemed safer than having to say they had me on their payroll. Eventually my friend Jeremy King from Benchmark Executive Search helped me land a full-time job with a start-up company.

While the investigation may have appeared to be quiet from the outside, it was anything but to many of those still at the Agency. Durham and his team had been vacuuming up documents, email, phone records, and other data relating to the tapes issue, which now spanned a period of over seven years. My former colleagues and subordinates were subjected to hour after hour of questioning by FBI agents who were second-guessing the meaning behind comments and notes made years before and continents away. As is so often the case in such matters, something said in an offhanded way years before is suddenly invested with huge import in retrospect. I felt terribly for my friends who were grilled. I knew the pressure they were under and also regretted that they were being pulled away from the effort to stop al-Qa'ida to engage in a microscopic examination of relatively trivial actions long past.

What was especially surreal for me was that I was not the one being questioned. Bob Bennett made clear to Durham's team that I was not going to bring the rope to my own lynching, so I was not an active participant in the investigation. We heard rumors that every document I had touched on any conceivably related matter was provided by the Agency to the FBI. I was convinced at the time, and remain convinced today, that if anything smacking of illegality had been found, Durham would have swiftly indicted me. Even if they had found something not directly relating to the tapes, they would have gone after me the way the Feds indicted Al Capone for tax evasion. Anything to make their point.

After a while I started hearing reports that friends, secretaries, former colleagues, and bosses of mine were being called to testify before a grand jury. Some were ordered to fly back to the United States multiple times from critical postings overseas in order to answer questions before the grand jury. The impression some came away with was that prosecutors were convinced something nefarious had been done; they were just struggling to figure out what and find the evidence.

My initial thought, back in late 2007, was that all this would blow over in a few months. But 2007 quickly became 2008. The cloud hung over me in 2009 and through much of 2010. On November 9, 2010, I was preparing to go to a business meeting when my cell phone rang. It was Bob Bennett. He had just received some news the traditional Washington way, via a leak. A reporter had called him with a tip that Special

Prosecutor Durham was going to announce that day that there would be no charges against me. I know enough to not believe every rumor floating around town, especially those that deliver news I want to believe. I thanked Bob and went ahead with my day. While I was at my meeting, however, Bennett called again. I stepped outside to hear what he had learned. Bennett told me he had just received a call from Durham confirming that I was not going to be charged. The word spread like wildfire among the CIA family. General Hayden, by this point a former CIA director, was still very well wired. He was traveling out West somewhere but was the first to get the news. He called me while running on a treadmill at a gym to congratulate me for having the cloud lifted from over my head.

Later that day, the Department of Justice issued a statement saying: "Mr. Durham has concluded that he will not pursue criminal charges for the destruction of the interrogation videotapes."

The timing was not a coincidence. November 9 was the fifth anniversary of the destruction of the tapes. It turned out that there was a statute-of-limitations issue. If the prosecutors could not build a viable case against me by that date, I was likely home free, at least regarding the initial act of ordering the destruction of the tapes.

While the nightmare was over for me, it was not for others. In August 2009 Eric Holder, attorney general in the new Obama administration, had expanded Durham's charter to include looking at the actions of CIA interrogators and contractors in matters beyond the tapes issue. Despite the fact that career prosecutors had looked at that in the previous administration and decided there were no prosecutable offenses, Holder placed those officers back under a cloud again.

After being under the gun for three years, you might think learning that you will not be prosecuted would be a moment for celebration. But more than a sense of relief, I felt it was an anticlimax. So much time and effort and angst had gone into dealing with the problem that a large part of me wanted simply to forget. I thanked Bennett profusely for his help and then called Patti to share the news. I don't think I was fully aware of how much pressure we both had felt until that moment. As I told her that the cloud had been lifted, we both began to cry tears of relief.

Chapter 9

WHAT WE DO

After all the talk about investigations and political double dealing, I wouldn't want a reader to walk away with the notion that life as a CIA officer is unpleasant. On the contrary, I enjoyed my thirty-one years as an Agency officer and would eagerly sign up to do it all over again if given the chance.

The lifestyle imposes its own burdens but is blessed with its unique rewards. I would not trade the experience for any other. In no other part of government am I aware of people being given the feeling of being part of a large team but also afforded so much individual responsibility. Agency officers share a great sense of camaraderie and often lighten the mood of tense responsibilities by pulling pranks on each other.

More than twenty years ago, I was chief of station in a Latin American country. The CIA had just gotten a new director (which seemed to be a regular occurrence at the time), and I got word that the boss wanted to pay a visit to my country. In calls and cable traffic from headquarters, I was told that the director felt it was crucial to the success of his trip to pay a call on the country's president. But when I contacted my local counterparts, I was told that unfortunately El Presidente was planning on being out of the country on the dates in question. The guys at headquarters were very unhappy with that news and told me that the director would be most disappointed. So I contacted the folks at the presidential palace again and, with all the political clout I could muster, convinced them to coax their boss into changing his schedule to accommodate me and my new leader.

A few weeks later the new DCI, whom I had never met, arrived in country. I went to the airport to meet him and waited at the bottom of the steps of his official aircraft. After shaking hands, the director said to me: "Thanks so much for arranging my visit. Unfortunately, my schedule is compressed and you'll need to cancel that visit with the president." My jaw hit the tarmac as I tried to maintain my composure. It was clear to me my influence in this country was also about to take a sudden dive. I was about to stammer something to the director when I heard raucous laughter from the top of the aircraft steps. The director's staff, knowing that I had used up every ounce of influence I had to get the country's president to stick around, had convinced the DCI to yank my chain with a bogus story about canceling the meeting. They had a good laugh at my expense.

I got them back. The director and his traveling party had been very interested in some intelligence that had come in suggesting that the country's president's much younger wife had recently been in close contact with her husband's political opposition. And when I say "close contact" I do not mean politically. During the course of his meeting with the president, the director got a chance to meet the first lady as well. He took quite a shine to her.

As the director and his team were getting ready to depart for Washington, I arranged for a car to arrive carrying a sealed envelope purportedly from the presidential palace for the departing CIA chief. I handed the envelope to him and wished him a safe trip. On the flight back to Washington he opened the envelope to find an autographed photo of the president along with a second autographed photo of the first lady with an inscription making clear that she looked forward to "close contact" with the DCI soon. After a suitable interval, I made sure the traveling party was made aware that neither inscription was genuine.

There was another memorable trip during the mid-1990s. Yet another new DCI decided he wanted to take a trip to Latin America to focus on U.S. efforts to work with host nations to slow drug trafficking. He brought a large entourage (including me) with him on a visit to Panama, Bolivia, and Colombia. When we got to Bogotá, Colombia, we were met by a motorcade of large white vans, which were intended to haul the official party to the hotel. The trip occurred shortly after a movie based on Tom Clancy's *Clear and Present Danger* hit the theaters. That film starts with a delegation of CIA officials arriving in Colombia and being taken in a motorcade of white SUVs straight into an ambush where most of them (other than Harrison Ford) are killed. The parallels to our circumstances were apparent to most of our party. Someone in the back of our van said, "Hey, I've seen this movie. It doesn't come out well." We debated which one of us was Harrison Ford.

Fortunately, we made it to our hotel safely and routine meetings ensued. A day later we were scheduled to visit Cali, where the infamous drug cartel had recently been taken down. Several members of our party were openly nervous about the risk of going there and called a late-night meeting to talk about the wisdom of taking the DCI into such a location. One of the senior analysts, who did not have a lot of operational experience, was particularly shaken. I was pretty sure that the Colombian government had the situation under control and had kept our visit quiet. But I couldn't resist playing on this guy's fears. "Yeah, those are some mean hombres there," I told him. "If they catch you they wrap you in explosives and throw you out of a helicopter. You explode on the way down and no one can find all the little pieces." He turned white and voted for immediately canceling that portion of the trip. Some of my more experienced colleagues were kicking me under the table for toying with the guy.

In the end, the trip went ahead as scheduled. We flew to Cali in very old Colombian helicopters. My nervous colleagues' eyes were as big as saucers and some of them claimed they saw old bullet holes in the helicopters. Nothing untoward happened. The trip was a success, although later that night Colombian TV had full coverage of our visit, including pictures of us at every stop, showing that it was not such a secret after all.

When I was chief of CTC, and later as head of the clandestine service, I did a lot of official travel. About once a year I had to travel to Moscow for counterterrorism exchanges with our Russian counterparts. It was my practice on such occasions to hit the gym in the Marriott Hotel we stayed at early on the morning after arrival in order to fight off jetlag with a full workout. On one of my last trips there I went to the gym as usual. It was a decent-size facility but empty except for me. Minutes after I started working out, however, one of the most beautiful women I have ever seen walked in. She was wearing skin-tight shorts and a sports bra, was exquisitely made up, and looked as if she had stepped out of a fashion magazine. Although the gym was expansive, she picked a piece of exercise equipment right next to mine and proceeded to work up quite a sweat while constantly looking directly at me and offering what I think they call in novels a "come hither" smile. There is no doubt in my mind that she was what the KGB used to call a "swallow," a beautiful woman dangled in front of an intelligence target with the hope of compromising him and recruiting him as their agent. When I started to feel weak, able to lift hardly any weights, I cut my workout short and headed back to my room—alone.

The Russians have never been subtle. They would frequently host counterterrorism meetings and invite senior intelligence officers from around the world, only to ignore and mistreat many of those in attendance who were from anywhere other than the largest and most powerful nations. I used to make it a point to seek out the officials they were clearly dissing and offer a hand of friendship to them. I did so out of a sense of human decency but admit that some of those officials whom I befriended after they were snubbed by the Russians later became quite helpful to the Agency.

There was another occasion when a delegation of Russian officers was visiting the United States for meetings with the CIA. As often happens in such cases, we were obliged to take our guests out to dinner when the day's meetings ended. Often you will accomplish more at a social event than you will during a day sitting across from each other in some conference room. This particular night we had taken the Russian delegation to a steak restaurant in Tysons Corner, Virginia, a few miles down the road from CIA headquarters. At one point one of the senior officers wanted to smoke. He was quite annoyed that American laws prevented lighting up at your table in the restaurant and that he was obliged to step outside. I decided to keep him company. As he took drags on his Ziganov high-nicotine cigarette, we made small talk. As he was finishing his smoke he asked about my ethnic background. I told him I was born in Puerto Rico. He seemed confused and surprised that someone who was not a WASP could be selected for such an important position. In thickly accented English he asked, "How do they trust you?" In his clumsy question, the Russian was wondering how an American of Latino descent could rise to the position of chief of the CIA's Counterterrorism Center. Looking him straight in the eye, I told him my assignment was as a result of my success in recruiting Russian intelligence officers to change sides. He was not amused.

Dealing with the Russians was quite a chore. They were always in the "receive mode," happy to take whatever information we were willing to share with them on terrorist threats but generally reluctant to offer much in return.

My first experience with them came only days after I joined CTC. It was shortly after 9/11 and a Russian delegation was in Washington for meetings. I was so new at the time that I could barely find my office in CTC. But I must have faked expertise well enough. Cofer Black, my boss in CTC, had little patience for Russian foot-dragging. Cofer attended one meeting and made quite a statement. He addressed the group with a stack of paper a couple of feet high in front of him. "This," he said, pointing to the pile of paper, "is the intelligence information the United States has shared with you." He picked up the stack and dropped it, creating an enormous boom. "And this," Cofer said, "is what we have gotten from you." He grabbed a small handful of papers and threw them in the air. The Russians watched a pitifully small number of documents float like feathers before silently hitting the table. While it was an impressive demonstration, it had little effect on subsequent performance.

Once I became chief of CTC, I was asked to attend twice-a-year meetings with the Russians. The leader of the U.S. delegation was Deputy Secretary of State Rich Armitage. Although I would have liked to avoid the meetings, since they produced little measurable result, Armitage insisted I go along. Perhaps he felt comfortable that, like Cofer, I would speak my mind, and when necessary was willing to launch stacks of paper into the Moscow skies.

Traveling overseas on official business was an important part of my duties. In my last job I spent about a week out of every month overseas. Generally, I passed up on traveling on big government jets and preferred low-key arrivals on commercial flights. Often I traveled alone or with a single aide. When I arrived in a foreign country, however, assuming that my visit was declared to the host government and they knew I was coming, I would get the red carpet treatment. Fixers from the host country intelligence service would meet me planeside and whisk me past the usual customs and immigration formalities. It was quite different coming home, however. When your name is Jose Rodriguez, I can assure you that it is hard to convince the TSA you don't bear special scrutiny. I almost never got back into the country without being pulled into secondary screening by earnest Homeland Security officials.

Getting back and forth to work while Stateside was less of an adventure. When you are undercover, as I was for most of my career, you are advised to vary your routes to work and engage in surveillance detection routes (called SDRs) to make sure you are not being followed. I admit that when I varied my path to and from work it generally had more to do with traffic conditions than it did with trying to avoid bad guys who might be trailing me.

Like the stereotypical spy, I do enjoy fast cars. Late in my career I purchased a Corvette, which I would drive to work with the top down on good-weather days. Shortly after I got the car, I was visiting one of the CIA's outlying buildings in the northern Virginia area. As I passed through the entry gate, a security barrier accidentally malfunctioned, popping up from the ground and wrecking the nose of my much-loved Vette. The folklore in the Office of Security is that the car was a total loss, but in truth they had to repair only a badly mangled front end. I was fortunate that I wasn't traveling the way I often did on weekends, on my motorcycle. A rogue security barrier under a Harley would not have been pretty.

One of the challenges of life as a CIA officer is maintaining a good balance between work and home life. Far too often I saw colleagues and subordinates get so wrapped up in defending the homeland that they paid too little attention to their own home front. Particularly when you are engaged in something as all-consuming as counterterrorism, it is easy to convince yourself that you are indispensable or that pulling an all-nighter at work can make the difference between life and death. During my time as head of CTC, I spent much, much more time trying to convince people to go home than I did explaining why they had to stay at work.

I was also a strong proponent of my officers' cluing their spouses in on their work. Many people at the Agency took the approach that our work was so secret that they couldn't share a whisper of what they did with the people closest too them. That is a big mistake. While you don't have to give away the most sensitive details of what you do, if you try to withhold everything from your spouse, and then disappear at odd hours for agent meetings, or depart on no notice for unexpected stretches of time, it won't be long before your mate will start wondering about the *real* nature of the secrets you are hiding. Operationally, it is also a good idea to let your spouse know where you are going in case you don't come back on time. That way he or she can alert your colleagues in the office so they can start searching for you.

It is unfair to keep so much of your life hidden from your spouse. Agency regulations permit its case officers to use discretion on what information to share, and I always encouraged my folks to lean toward openness. Patti was always a huge asset to my career. Ambassadors, diplomats, foreign officials, and even presidents and dictators always loved her. With her charm, intelligence, and good looks, she would disarm them, and they loved having her around. As a result, we were invited to many events that made it easier for me to do my job—collect intelligence. Patti is a wonderful hostess and made people feel comfortable when they visited our home, and they always wanted to come back. But she is also very insightful about people and would often caution me about those who she sensed were shady or could not be trusted.

Traveling with Patti made my life easier, too. Whenever

we went through an airport, if she was along I would breeze through customs and immigration. But when flying by myself I was often singled out and harassed.

I was on the road so much and so consumed with work that a very heavy burden on the home front fell on Patti. She was chief of station at home taking care of the children, our finances, our real estate, and other challenges. I was blessed that she was always supportive of my career and cheerfully followed me (kids in tow) to some dangerous, unhealthy, and unsavory places.

I would never have been able to achieve half of the success I did without her.

Another tricky part of life undercover is what to share with your kids—and when. While you can expect a spouse to understand the need for operational cover, you can't count on a child to be able to resist blurting out your true employer during "show and tell" time at the elementary school. Agency families carefully judge when their kids are old enough to be let in on the secret of what Mom or Dad does for a living and to be counted on to help maintain the cover.

In our case, we broke the news to our boys that their dad was in the CIA when they each were about twelve years old. You have to handle those conversations carefully. There are stories around the Agency of similar revelations that, at least initially, didn't go down so well. One father explained to his son that he was "sort of a spy," to which the boy responded, "You mean we are Russian?" In my case, I made sure both sons understood I was working on behalf of the U.S.A. When I broke cover with my oldest son, Nic, and told him I really worked for the CIA, he said: "Cool, Pop, is your name really Jose Rodriguez?" The timing of revealing my true line of work with our second son, Alec, was not entirely of my choosing. This was when we were in Mexico and a major local publication put my name and affiliation on the cover of their news magazine. He was a little confused by the situation at first, but both boys were proud of their pop's career and success at the CIA.

When most people think about the CIA, they don't reflect on family matters. Usually the images that come to mind are quite different. I get it. The actions that my colleagues and I took in the war on terrorism are highly controversial. When you are working for a clandestine organization, fighting a shadowy enemy, what you did and didn't do will inevitably be shrouded in mystery and misperception.

I feel an obligation, however, to try to penetrate that fog and frontally address many of the ethical, moral, and practical questions that critics, pundits, friends, and enemies have raised. There is far too much misinformation out there, leading good people to leap to the wrong conclusions about our activities. Part of the problem is that much of the conventional wisdom, the things that "everybody knows," is wrong.

The best way to deal with this is for me to address some of the fundamental questions and accusations that I get from those who wish to second-guess what we did. The questions range from baseline questions about who we are and the principles we are trying to protect and defend, to those that focus on the practicalities and effectiveness of our tactics.

If you were to sum up the overarching question about this period that we receive from our critics, it might be stated in three words: "How could you?" How could you torture fellow human beings? The question stems from one of the most fundamentally incorrect "everyone knows" statements. "Everyone knows what you did was torture." Wrong.

Let there be no doubt. The treatment that a small handful of terrorists received at our hands was unpleasant. It was unpleasant for them and, not insignificantly, unpleasant for us. But we went to great lengths to make sure that it was legal, safe, and effective. We went to the seniormost legal officials in our government and asked, demanded really, legal rulings in writing of what could be done without crossing the line. We went back to those officials several times to ask for reaffirmation, and during one period in 2004 when some of the officials wavered, we suspended the program until we received assurances that we were on solid legal ground.

In recent years some outside legal scholars, and those who pretend to be, have challenged the legal judgments of those who authorized the enhanced interrogation program. That is their right, but the men and women of the intelligence community don't have the ability or luxury of shopping around for legal opinions. The Department of Justice senior officials who provided our guidelines are sometimes accused of telling us what we wanted to hear. But those officials, at the top of the food chain for U.S. government lawyers, gave us their best judgments and we had no reason to believe they were incorrect, then or now.

Whether or not the EIT program was legal, many critics argue that it was unnecessary because we could have obtained the same information using traditional interrogation techniques. Some disgruntled FBI special agents in particular push this notion. Could we have gotten the same information using typical FBI practices? Maybe. If we had all the time in the world, perhaps we could have. But we did not. You cannot overstate the urgency that we felt about getting answers quickly. The small number of people who were subjected to the EIT program were among the few people in the world who had in their heads information that we *knew* could stop another, possibly imminent, devastating attack that might rival 9/11 in scale. Typical law enforcement interrogation tactics are designed to unravel who committed past crimes and to gather evidence that can be used in a court of law to punish the guilty. We knew who had committed the past crime, and while taking the surviving senior al-Qa'ida leadership to trial would be somewhat satisfying, we were much more focused on stopping the next attack.

It is important to note that we are not claiming universal applicability for EITs. We implemented the program specifically for *these* terrorists, in *these* circumstances, and for *this* period of time. We chose not to get into an argument with theorists who say that rapport building is the best or only way to go. From their point of view, EITs could not work in theory. Our position was: Your theories are irrelevant. The techniques worked in practice.

The typical criminal whom law enforcement deals with bears little resemblance to the kinds of people we were handling. A drug lord in a cartel pushes narcotics not because heroin is a religion to him; he does so to make a profit. So when captured, he may be motivated to cooperate in the hope of receiving a reduced sentence, favorable treatment for his family, or some other carrot. A senior al-Qa'ida operative, on the other hand, is part of a jihad. He is not looking for favors and in fact generally would welcome being made a martyr. Many dismiss any thought of their family's future comfort, saying that their fate is in Allah's hands. They have been trained to resist interrogation and consider it a major victory if they can hold out just long enough for another major attack that they were privy to to be carried out.

Sure, some critics say, eventually you can get anyone to talk, but when they do so they will be saying whatever they need to say to get the pain and discomfort to stop. To start with, it is important to remember that the interrogation tactics are not about pain. If they were designed to inflict pain on the detainee, there are many other ways that could be done. (In the days immediately after 9/11, the CIA received communications from hundreds of average Americans wanting to do what they could to help us punish al-Qa'ida for its acts. I remember one letter we received from one person who wrote: "I'm a dentist. Trust me, I can inflict pain.") Rather than to inflict pain, our goal was to induce a sense of hopelessness in the detainees. We wanted them to quickly reach the conclusion that withholding information from us was folly and that we already knew a lot of information and would eventually learn the rest, so they might as well cooperate now to avoid a lot of unnecessary discomfort.

Regarding the allegation that we "tortured" people until they "would say anything to get us to stop," one of my former colleagues said: "What bothers me is that our critics not only believe we are evil, they think we are stupid."

The people who were asking the questions, and the people who were analyzing the answers, were among the leading experts on al-Qa'ida in the world. Often they knew the answers to questions before they were asked. Always they double-checked the information six ways from Sunday before accepting it as credible. As we got more and more al-Qa'ida leaders in custody, we were able to play one off against the other. We would ask a question, get a response, and then say, "Oh, really? That's not what KSM said, he said X." We would ask factual questions, such as "Where did you travel to in 1999?" When the detainee said, "Nowhere," we would say, "No, actually you went to Tanganyika and stayed at the Hill Top Hotel." They quickly learned not to mislead us. Still, we never assumed that what a detainee was telling us was true. But after you caught them in a few lies, and the specter of renewed EITs (which they didn't know we were very unlikely to return to) arose in their minds, they generally gave you something close enough to the truth.

After a while, our debriefers got to know the detainees extremely well. One of the detainees had the habit of licking his lips right before engaging in a fabrication. When asked a question one day, he said, "Well," and then exhibited the "tell" by licking his lips. His debriefer stopped him before going on and said, "This is where you are about to lie to me, isn't it?" The detainee hung his head and mumbled, "Yes." After a pause, he went on to answer truthfully.

Another of the common errors is the assumption that detainees were subjected to enhanced interrogation for months or years on end. Or the belief that every time we came up with a new question, if the detainee didn't tell us what we wanted to hear, we subjected him to harsh treatment all over again.

In fact, most of the detainees in CIA custody received *none* of the EITs. Only about thirty out of one hundred or so were subjected to any of the techniques. The techniques stopped as soon as the detainee became compliant and agreed to cooperate. And in virtually every case, they never again were subjected to EITs. Of these thirty detainees who received any EITs, only three—let me say that again, three—were ever waterboarded. Even for those three who went through most if not all of the EITs before being waterboarded, the entire time between first being asked if they wanted to cooperate and refusing, through the use of escalating procedures up to waterboarding, took a matter of as little as seven to at most less than thirty days.

Even for those critics who understood that the EITs were not applied for a lengthy period, there was often a lack of understanding of their continuing benefit. For example, following the death of Usama bin Ladin in May 2011, a National Security Council spokesman implied that EITs did not contribute to UBL's demise because much of the intelligence on his whereabouts came long after the EITs stopped. Hello! That is the way it is supposed to work.

We never suggested that the EITs would be a panacea. Once detainees became compliant, that did not mean that they would tell us everything they knew. They would still try to protect their most cherished secrets. But they told us much, much more than they would have otherwise, and, often unwittingly, they gave us insights that unlocked the mysteries we wanted to unravel most. During one debriefing session, one of our people asked a senior detainee, "What is it you fear most about these sessions?" After thinking for a moment, he responded: "I am afraid I might inadvertently tell you something which leads to the capture of the Sheikh" (Usama bin Ladin). Well, all right then, we have a place to start.

The detainees were always trying to game the system. At one point we discovered that KSM was trying to signal his fellow detainees (using a method I cannot describe). In one message he instructed another detainee to "tell them nothing about the courier." Short of giving us a name, you couldn't ask for a better tipoff.

Why didn't the detainees simply give up UBL's location when they became compliant? Two reasons: Most of them had no idea where he was and all of them tried mightily to protect that information. They did, however, provide us bits of information that, over the period of years, allowed targeting analysts to determine that the use of couriers would be the key to finding bin Ladin, and they provided us the alias of the main courier, which eventually led to the determination of his true name and location.

One of the most frustrating charges is the one that goes something like this: "Waterboarding must not work; otherwise you would not have had to do it to KSM 183 times and to Abu Zubaydah 83." The charge is frustrating for a number of reasons, not the least of which is that the CIA's own inspector general created the canard. It is a measure of the care and precision with which we conducted the program that Agency officers recorded every drip of water that was used in the waterboard process. In some of the fanciful simulations and animations used by the critics to illustrate the process, they show huge buckets of water or fully charged hoses being used. In fact the water was dispensed in short splashes from ordinary plastic water bottles. Each time the bottle was tipped counted as one application. So the "183 times" that we get credited/blamed for waterboarding KSM in fact involved only 183 splashes of water (applications).

According to a 2007 International Committee on the Red Cross report, which has been publicly released, Abu Zubaydah said he was subjected to waterboarding "during five sessions of ill-treatment [the ICRC's word] that took place during an approximately one-week intense period of interrogation allegedly in Afghanistan in 2002. During each session, apart from one, the suffocation technique was applied once or twice, on one occasion it was applied three times."

KSM is quoted in the ICRC report as saying that he, too, had been waterboarded only five times. In this instance, KSM was much closer to the truth than the CIA IG. My information is that each session lasted an average of less than 4.5 minutes.

Keep in mind that captured al-Qa'ida training manuals instruct their operatives to exaggerate any supposed abuse they might suffer at the hands of captors. In this case, the CIA IG did their work for them.

"Well, it doesn't matter!" critics often say. "Even if it were only a single occasion, it is a cruel and barbarous act bringing the detainees to the brink of death from drowning or asphyxiation." Again, not true. The technique gives detainees the *sensation* of being on the verge of drowning, but they are in no danger of doing so. The exposure to pouring water was almost always brief (most less than ten seconds a pour) and always intensely supervised by a number of Agency people, including at least one with medical training. This last statement often produces another outcry. "What? Medically trained individuals took part? This is a violation of their oaths!" Nonsense. Imagine if one of the three—remember, only three—individuals had suffered some sort of health problem while the procedure was going on, and we did not have medical personnel present. We would have been excoriated for our failure to have someone standing by who could have immediately dealt with any medical crisis, including those that might be entirely unrelated to waterboarding.

The flip side to the question, why did you waterboard so much, is: "If it worked, why did you stop the practice entirely in 2003?" What people need to remember is that we used waterboarding only in the rarest of circumstances. We used it on senior detainees who had just been captured, who refused to cooperate, and who we had reason to believe were knowledgeable about future al-Qa'ida attacks that might come at any moment. Those circumstances did not repeat themselves in 2004–06. We felt we were able to get the information we needed and the information newly captured detainees had by using lesser techniques.

It will come as a shock to some of our critics to read this, but I believe we did make some mistakes in coming up with the EITs. One of the biggest errors was in labeling our most aggressive technique "waterboarding." By doing so, we made it easy for those who find fault with our tactics to allege that what we did for those three al-Qa'ida leaders was the same as the atrocities conducted by Japanese soldiers in World War II, and by others, going back hundreds of years. The goals, techniques, and application of Japanese waterboarding were entirely different from the carefully managed and applied procedures we used with these three terrorists.

The opponents of the EIT program will say, "We don't care what you call it. Everyone knows it was torture!" The "everyone" who "know" this are wrong. If it was torture, then was it torture when the tactic was used in training literally thousands of U.S. military personnel? If the CIA's waterboarding was torture, why weren't the U.S. military personnel who conducted this training charged with crimes? Because while the procedure is harsh and unpleasant, it does not cross the line into what can legitimately be called torture. Critics will argue that it is all a matter of intent. U.S. military personnel undergoing training presumably know in the back of their minds that they are taking part in an exercise that will end before long. But I am told that those taking part quickly find the technique *very* real and quickly abandon any thought that it is a game. The reason the U.S. Air Force dropped waterboarding from its repertoire of tactics in training was not that their personnel dismissed it as just a simulation, but that they found it impossible to resist.

Waterboarding is not a trivial event. It is something that no one would look forward to enduring themselves. Sometime after the use of waterboarding became generally known and when it was subject to intense public debate, one U.S. senator decided that he wanted to find out for himself how it felt. Bill Nelson, the senior senator from Florida, told the Agency that he wanted to be subjected to the tactic so he could decide whether it amounted to torture. While I admire his commitment to fact-finding, the Agency decided it would not be wise to accommodate the senator's thirst for knowledge. Despite the fact that he appeared to be in great shape, the senator, who had flown on the Space Shuttle *Columbia* in 1986, was in his mid-sixties at the time of his request. Even though we would have had medical personnel standing by, we wondered what would happen if he suffered a cardiac event during the experiment. Bad enough the CIA might be blamed for killing a U.S. senator, *this* Democratic senator was from Florida. If he had tragically died, his successor would have been appointed by the Republican governor at the time, Jeb Bush, the president's brother. The conspiracy theorists would have gone wild.

There is another group of skeptics who refuse to believe the rationale I give for why I believed the destruction of the interrogation videotapes was urgent and necessary. They won't accept any answer other than their imagined one: that we were covering up evidence of dastardly deeds. The truth, as I have said over and over again, is that my goal was to protect the identities of my officers.

Why didn't you just blur the faces of those shown on the tapes? I am sometimes asked. The answer is simple. While al-Qa'ida may not have the capability in-house, there are countless techies in the world who like nothing better than unraveling secrets, and it wouldn't have been long before the full, unobscured images of those CIA officers would have been available for anyone with an internet connection.

Is there any doubt that al-Qa'ida would like to retaliate against CIA personnel? Some of our critics would be happy to take a chance that they wouldn't, but I would never make that bet with someone else's safety. This is not just theory.

In 2008 several news organizations got the name of an outstanding former CIA officer who was involved in the Abu Zubaydah and KSM cases. The officer was not undercover at the time, but connecting him to such significant actions posed considerable risk to him and his family. The *New York Times* in particular was very aggressive about trying to get this officer to talk to them to describe details of the interrogation of senior al-Qa'ida members. They tracked down his home address and, unannounced, on a Sunday morning, a reporter came knocking on his door. When no one answered, he slipped a note in his door. The reporter then drove down the street and parked and watched the house for a couple of hours. He then contacted the officer's mother, his sister, and a high school friend. The message left with each of them was, tell him we want to help him tell his story—a story he wasn't looking to tell. The *New York Times* said they already knew a lot about this guy and were planning on running a story, with or without his help, describing his activities and naming him.

He was feeling mightily harassed. So I helped facilitate the support of my lawyer, Bob Bennett, who contacted the *Times* telling them to back off. The *Times* wouldn't hear of it. To them, this was a story about a guy who was very successful at deriving information from what we were learning from KSM after the EITs were applied—suggesting that the EITs had nothing to do with our success. They wanted to make him a hero and couldn't understand why he would not want to be named. In fact, he is a hero and would tell you that it was only because KSM had become compliant and begun to freely share information that CIA officers were able to connect as many dots as they did.

CIA director General Mike Hayden took time out from a ceremony marking his retirement from the air force after thirty-nine years of service to call the *Times* and urge them to keep the name out of the paper. They didn't think he was serious enough or made a compelling argument and they ran with the name anyway.

Concerned that the unwanted publicity might put him and his family in jeopardy, the officer contacted the Agency office of security, which told him they couldn't do much for him until there was evidence that someone was trying to harm him. If it got to that point, he figured, it might well be too late.

He ran up substantial legal fees (and keep in mind that no

one ever accused him of doing anything wrong). Much later the Agency reimbursed him—but that was never a sure thing.

A year after the story first appeared in the *New York Times,* the former officer got a call from the Agency's Counterintelligence Center. They said, "We need you to come in to headquarters—now!" They told him that the *New York Times* article naming him had gotten to KSM's cell in Guantanamo Bay within two weeks of publication. But more recently, and much more troubling, officials in GITMO had found photographs of CIA officers in the possession of detainees at the prison. The photos were clearly taken surreptitiously, and included pictures taken outside their homes and entering their workplaces. Reportedly, the "John Adams Project," an ACLU-run operation, had been stalking current and former CIA officers and taking pictures of them to show to al-Qa'ida detainees. It would not take much of an imagination to think that those photos might find their way into the hands of nondetained terrorists. So when people ask why I thought it necessary to work so hard to protect the identity of CIA officers, the answer is that it was not just al-Qa'ida I was protecting them from but also from the efforts of the *New York Times* and the ACLU, which, unwittingly, might aid and abet al-Qa'ida.

When they tire of arguing that the CIA's interrogation program was "evil," our critics resort to the claim that we got nothing of value from it anyway. As former CIA director General Mike Hayden puts it, people have the right to say they don't want their government using these techniques, they have the right to their views, but claiming that they didn't work, "That's mine," Hayden says. He, his predecessors, and his successors know they did work.

Almost every critic who dismisses the results of the EIT

program is someone who did not then and does not now have access to the full output of the interrogation from the detainees. Even some who would claim they were totally aware of the results of the post-EIT terrorist debriefing, such as some former FBI agents, are lying or deluded.

What I can swear to you, as head of CTC at the time, and what every one of the people working under me implementing the program would tell you, is that we have never in our careers ever seen such important, critical, and lifesaving intelligence come from any other program.

"Sure," some will say, "you guys are just trying to justify your actions, which were nothing less than war crimes." As I have explained, we very carefully sought and received legal counsel before entering into this program. We don't need to sugarcoat anything. If the program had been ineffective, we could easily say, "We were grasping at straws in a time of great urgency. We now recognize there are better ways to do things and won't make the same mistake." Given the pressure of political correctness, that would be the easiest thing in the world to say. No one likes to be labeled a "torturer" or a potential "war criminal." It would be easy to cave, to take the position that "mistakes were made." It would also be easy to point fingers elsewhere, saying, for example, that we were pressured by politicians. It would be easy, and it would be wrong.

In February 2009, the Senate Intelligence Committee announced plans to conduct a thorough review of the CIA's detention and interrogation program. Six months later the Republicans on the committee revealed that they would no longer take part in the inquiry because Attorney General Holder had reopened criminal investigation of some people who had been involved in the program. Later, some of the members added to their reasons for not participating the statement that they believed that the investigation was being politicized. At this writing, two and a half years after the investigation was supposedly started, nothing has come of it. I do not know if there ever will be a conclusion to the study, but given the partisan rancor that has enveloped it, I have little hope for the objectivity or accuracy of such a conclusion.

Honorable people can come to the conclusion that although the EITs were successful, they are not something they want their government to engage in. I totally respect that point of view. But if people want to adopt that stance, they need to complete the thought. They need to articulate that not only do they not want their government to engage in these practices, but they are willing to accept that hundreds, thousands, and perhaps more innocent people might die at the hands of terrorists because their government was directed not to use these controversial techniques, no matter the results. It is because it is so hard to say, "I am willing to let thousands of people die to avoid giving people like KSM a few minutes of discomfort" that so many of our critics work so hard to deny that any useful information comes from the EITs.

Another frequent argument that we encounter is that by engaging in the EIT program we have somehow legitimized for current and future opponents the right to similarly treat captured U.S. military personnel. "How would you feel," we are asked, "if some country, such as Iran, were to waterboard U.S. special operations forces troops they somehow got their hands on?" The circumstances are in no way analogous. To start with, legitimate military personnel are covered by the Geneva Conventions, whereas terrorists, such as those al-Qa'ida leaders we held, are not. There is a vast difference between a soldier carrying out the orders of his country and a mass murderer intent on inflicting horrific casualties on members of the public.

If Iranians were to capture some ununiformed civilian who had already murdered three thousand innocent civilians in their homeland and was intent on murdering thousands more, they might be able to make a case for harsh interrogation. But that is not going to happen. Rogue regimes have never needed an excuse to abuse genuine prisoners of war, and, sadly, they will probably continue to do so in the future without need to rely on the EIT program as a precedent. Beyond legitimate foreign governments, the argument about how the EITs might influence future actions of terrorist groups is an absurdity. The people who happily order colleagues to fly airliners into packed office towers and joyfully cut the heads off American journalists and contractors need no motivation to step up their brutality.

The final accusation I would like to deal with is the notion that we hid our activities at black sites, aboard clandestine rendition aircraft, and elsewhere because we were ashamed of what we did. On the contrary, the people involved, almost to a man and woman, have told me that they were extraordinarily proud of what we did. They had never before felt such an enormous sense of responsibility, nor had they participated in any other program that contributed so much to protecting the safety of Americans and our allies around the world. We kept the program secret (or more accurately, *tried* to do so) because it needed to be secret to be effective. Those who worked hard to expose it have made it easier for America's enemies to succeed.

Chapter 10

THE CIA UNDER OBAMA

After retiring from the Agency in January 2008, and especially after being given the "all clear" sign by the special prosecutor in November 2010, I have tried to get on with my life. But you never completely get past or get over a lifetime spent at the CIA. There are always constant reminders of past successes, failures, and controversies.

While those reminders are continual, they come with greater frequency during political years. For better or worse, and it is almost always worse, the conduct of U.S. intelligence has become a political football. It was no different in the 2008 presidential campaign when the Republican candidate, John McCain, an outspoken critic of the CIA's terrorist detention practices, was outdone by his Democratic opponent, Barack Obama, who was even more vocal in condemning us.

Writing in *Foreign Affairs* magazine in 2007, Obama called for building a "better, freer, world" and said that meant "ending the practices of shipping away prisoners in the dead of the night to be tortured in far-off countries, of detaining thousands without charge or trial, or maintaining a network of secret prisons to jail people beyond the reach of the law."

Immediately after winning election, Obama appeared on CBS News' *60 Minutes* and said: "I intend to close Guantanamo, and I will follow through on that. I have said repeatedly that America doesn't torture. And I'm gonna make sure that we don't torture. Those are part and parcel of an effort to regain America's moral stature in the world."

In December 2008, President-elect Obama met with CIA

director Mike Hayden, who traveled to Chicago to brief him on the realities of our interrogation program. The program by that time had been vastly scaled back. Hayden carefully explained how extraordinarily productive the EITs had been and gave a demonstration of how mild the remaining interrogation techniques were by having one of his aides stand up to be slapped and held the way an al-Qa'ida operative might be. The impression that Hayden and his group got was that Obama and his transition team were surprised that the techniques still in use were so mild. When the new administration launched, however, one of Obama's first acts, on January 22, 2009, was to sign a sweeping executive order requiring that only the interrogation guidelines in the Army Field Manual be observed in the interrogation of any detainees in U.S. custody. He ordered the CIA to close all existing detention facilities and prohibited it from operating detention facilities in the future. He signed another executive order mandating the closure of the Guantanamo Bay detention facility within one year.

About ten days later, Obama's nominee to be director of the Central Intelligence Agency, Leon Panetta, appeared before the Senate Intelligence Committee for his confirmation hearing and declared that in the past the CIA had sent detainees to other countries to be tortured. When pressed on the matter, Panetta admitted he had not been briefed on such a program. Apparently it was just another one of those things that "everybody knows"—even if they are wrong.

In response to a question, Panetta flatly called waterboarding "torture." He did add, "If I had a ticking bomb situation and obviously whatever was being used I felt was not sufficient, I would not hesitate to go to the president of the United States and request whatever additional authority I would need."

On April 16, 2009, the president announced that his Justice Department was releasing that day a series of memos produced between 2002 and 2005 laying out the previous administration's legal justification for the use of interrogation techniques against terrorism suspects. He said that there was no choice but to release the documents, since they were subject to a court case, and besides the interrogation tactics "undermine our moral authority and do not make us safer." He said the country must "reject the false choice between our security and our ideals." He went on to assure those who carried out their duties relying in good faith on the DOJ memos that they would not be subject to prosecution. It was, he said, time to move forward from this "dark and painful chapter in our history."

The president then took his crusade overseas to undo what he saw as the errors of the past. In June 2009 he traveled to Cairo, where he made a speech to the Arab world in which he declared: "9/11 was an enormous trauma to our country. The fear and anger that it provoked was understandable, but in some cases, it led us to act contrary to our ideals. We are taking concrete actions to change course. I have unequivocally prohibited the use of torture by the United States, and I have ordered the prison at Guantanamo Bay closed by early next year."

I cannot tell you how disgusted my former colleagues and I felt to hear ourselves labeled "torturers" by the president of the United States. To hear that we had acted contrary to American ideals was infuriating. The words of the president and of members of his staff have consequences. Members of the CIA and officials from the previous administration, all the way up to the former president, are threatened with arrest in some foreign locales as war criminals. While such action is unlikely, the chances increase when those seeking to prosecute them have to look no further than the words of the current president for support.

In August of 2009 the new attorney general, Eric Holder, announced his intention to reopen criminal investigations of

CIA officers who had been involved in incidents involving the interrogation of detainees. Holder made the decision despite the fact that career Department of Justice lawyers (not political appointees) had closed the investigations during the previous administration, finding that no prosecutions were warranted. The CIA itself was the organization that first reported these incidents to DOJ, out of an abundance of caution. They included such things as Agency officers blowing cigar smoke in the face of detainees. Other incidents reported were considerably more serious, including the deaths of two detainees who were not part of the interrogation program run by CTC.

Holder eventually admitted that he had not even read the reports by career DOJ attorneys (in which they explained why they declined to prosecute) before deciding to reopen the cases. A few weeks later, seven former CIA directors, who had served during both Democratic and Republican administrations, wrote to Obama urging him to "exercise [his] authority to reverse Attorney General Holder's" decision. Their plea was ignored.

The Obama administration seemed to have a political stake in declaring the actions of the past evil and their own actions necessary and correct. My former CIA colleague John Brennan is now deputy national security advisor and assistant to the president. Back in 2007, however, he was out of government and a consultant for CBS News. In November of that year he told CBS anchor Harry Smith that enhanced interrogation techniques had borne fruit. Brennan said: "There have been a lot of information that has come out from these interrogation procedures that the Agency has in fact used against the real hard-core terrorists. It has saved lives. And let's not forget, these are hardened terrorists who have been responsible for 9/11, who have shown no remorse at all for the deaths of three thousand innocents." Brennan went on in his CBS interview to defend Michael Mukasey, who at the time was undergoing confirmation hearings as the Bush administration's attorney general, for refusing to call waterboarding "torture." Had Mukasey done so, Brennan explained, those "who authorized and actually used this type of procedure may be subject to some type of judicial action." He was right, but he is singing a different tune today.

In August 2009, the administration created an outfit they called the High-Value Detainee Interrogation Group, or HIG, which is supposed to combine the expertise of the FBI, the CIA, the DOD, and other agencies in interrogating top terrorists—should we ever capture any. They placed the unit under the supervision of the National Security Council, ensuring that if any controversy ever arises again about detainee interrogation, the blame will land squarely and immediately on the White House doorstep.

Five months later Umar Farouk Abdulmutallab, the underwear bomber, through dumb luck, failed to detonate his bomb. Had he succeeded, he might have brought down a commercial airliner over Detroit. Who put him up to the mission? Were there others like him out there? What other tactics was al-Qa'ida considering? All important questions, but the HIG wasn't called in to interrogate him, for what turned out to be a good reason—the administration hadn't quite gotten around to making the unit operational. Instead, the attorney general jumped in and authorized officials on scene to read the potential bomber his Miranda rights after being questioned for mere minutes.

The odd thing is that the Obama administration has been very aggressive in going after al-Qa'ida and other terrorists. In many ways it has taken the efforts of the past administration and built upon them. I applaud it for that. But by its precipitous actions to ban any interrogation techniques beyond those in the Army Field Manual, its rush to bar any overseas detention facility, and its stumbling efforts to close Guantanamo Bay (only to have that effort put on hold when it discovered no viable alternative to that prison for the worst al-Qa'ida operatives), the Obama administration has managed to tie itself into knots when it comes to dealing with terrorists. It has given a road map to America's enemies. Al-Qa'ida now knows exactly how far (not very) the United States will go in interrogating its prisoners. They have a manual on how to wait us out and live to strike again.

If an al-Qa'ida operative were to be captured in Pakistan today, that person would likely be held in Pakistani custody. Ask yourself, is that detainee better off because of this administration's changes? Is the United States better off? One gets the clear impression that capturing and interrogating terrorists is on the "too hard" list these days.

With no black sites still open and no reasonable place to take detainees who might be captured, the administration has stumbled into a "take no prisoners" approach. It has limited itself to using blunt instruments in the war on terror. An administration that thinks it was "torture" to interfere with the sleep cycle of a handful of the worst terrorists on the planet has no problem with authorizing the firing of Hellfire missiles into a group of thirty or forty suspects gathered around a campfire. Care is taken, no doubt, to try to keep collateral damage to a minimum, but sadly, from time to time there will inevitably be innocents in the wrong place at the wrong time. The administration is left with the vague hope that God shields those who mistakenly venture too close to the real enemy. Needless to say, there is no opportunity to interrogate or learn anything from a suspect who is vaporized by a missile launched by a keystroke executed thousands of miles away.

I have the impression that some of the savvier members of

the Obama administration's national security team are start-ing to recognize that they have boxed themselves in. How to get out of that box is something they haven't figured out yet, however.

General David Petraeus had spoken out against the en-hanced interrogation techniques when he was serving in top military positions. But when he had his Senate confirmation hearing in June 2011, I thought I detected a subtle shift in his position. While he continued to support the use of the Army Field Manual for interrogations, he was asked by Senator John McCain about the "ticking time bomb" scenario.

Here is what he said: "I think that is a special case. I think there should be discussion of that by policymakers and by Congress. I think that it should be thought out ahead of time." Later, in an exchange with Senator McCain, Petraeus said that he believed this should be "a nuclear football kind of procedure where . . . there is an authorization, but it has to come from the top . . . this can't be something where we are forcing low-level individuals to have to make a choice under enormous duress." I would submit that that was pretty much where we were in 2002. We very much heard the time bomb ticking. No low-level individuals made any decisions. At the highest level of the U.S. government a set of tactics was approved and carefully and selectively implemented.

Well, what about Petraeus's caveat that this be discussed by policymakers and Congress? Once again, I would argue that that is what we did.

In May 2009, amid the Obama administration's efforts to demonize the actions of the past, Speaker of the House Nancy Pelosi stood up and accused the CIA of lying to her and her colleagues about our interrogation program. That simply wasn't so. As I said earlier, I was the one who led a CIA team to Capi-tol Hill to brief Pelosi and Porter Goss, then chairman of the

House Intelligence Committee, on September 4, 2002. We described in detail each of the specific techniques used in the interrogation of AZ that had been used for a couple of weeks in August. We explained that as a result of the techniques, Abu Zubaydah was compliant and providing good intelligence. We made it crystal clear that authorized techniques, including waterboarding, had by then been used on Abu Zubaydah. Years later Pelosi said that we only briefly mentioned waterboarding but had left the impression that it had not been used. That is untrue. Neither she nor Goss posed any objection to the techniques that were then in use. I *know* she got it. There is no doubt in my mind that she, like almost all Americans less than a year after 9/11, wanted us to be aggressive to make sure that al-Qa'ida wasn't able to replicate their attack.

One of the members of the small team of people I brought with me from CTC mentioned in the course of the briefing that there was another technique that had been considered but had not been authorized and had not been used. Pelosi piped up immediately and said that in her view use of that technique (which I will not describe here) would have been "wrong." I agree. That is why we didn't use it. But since she felt free to label one considered-and-rejected technique as wrong, we went away with the clear impression that she harbored no such feelings about the ten tactics that we told her were in use.

Six days after the session with Goss and Pelosi, a cable went out from headquarters to the black site informing them that the briefing for the House leadership had taken place (a similar briefing for Senate Intelligence Committee officials was conducted on September 27). The cable to the field made clear that Goss and Pelosi had been briefed on the state of AZ's interrogation, specifically including the use of the waterboard and other enhanced interrogation techniques.

Seven years later, when the winds, and the administration,

had changed, Pelosi told the world that the CIA had lied to her. Porter Goss, always the gentleman, wrote an Op-Ed piece for the *Washington Post* in which he described the comments coming from the Hill as a "disturbing epidemic of amnesia." He reported that it was not a single briefing but "an ongoing subject with lots of back and forth between those members and the briefers." He said he was "slack-jawed" to hear that some members claimed not to know what was going on.

So Pelosi was another member of Congress reinventing the truth. What's the big deal? The problem is the message they are sending to the men and women of the intelligence community who to this day are being asked to undertake dangerous and sometimes controversial actions on behalf of their government. They are told that the administration and Congress "have their back." You will forgive CIA officers if they are not filled with confidence. I sometimes think that many politicians had watched too many episodes of the old TV series *Mission Impossible*. The part they liked best was the opening, in which the operatives were told that if anything went wrong their leaders would "disavow any knowledge of your actions." That is not how it should work in the real world. It is no accident that one of the busiest outfits in Washington is the firm that sells legal liability insurance to CIA officers in case they find themselves hauled into court facing charges for doing things that this administration, or the one before it, and this Congress, or the one before that, ordered them to do.

The seeds that the Obama administration has sown have already begun to bear fruit. Unable or unwilling to capture, hold, and interrogate terrorists, it has, in my view, over-relied on technical means to kill suspected terrorists from afar. Drones can be a highly effective way of dealing with high-priority targets who cannot be reached any other way. But they should not become the drug of choice for an administration that is afraid to use successful, legal, and safe tactics of the past. Go to the well too often with drones and you alienate the fragile partners we have in those areas where potential targets abound.

It has been widely reported that the administration used remotely piloted vehicles to kill Anwar al-Awlaki, an American citizen, in Yemen on September 30, 2011. At least two other people reportedly died with him, including another American, Samir Khan, whose presence with al-Awlaki may have been unknown to those ordering the shot. Let me be clear: Al-Awlaki was an evil man who had close ties to 9/11 hijackers and helped inspire the murderous rampage of the Fort Hood shooter and the nearly successful actions of the underwear bomber. Al-Awlaki's removal from the gene pool was a positive thing.

Although it is not a word I would ever use, there is a German term, *Schadenfreude*, which means taking pleasure from the misfortune of others. I must admit a small case of it as I observe the current administration facing some challenges not unlike those we faced not that long ago. Suddenly members of Congress (mostly from the opposing party) are demanding public release of secret Justice Department memos that lay out the justification for the actions just taken. The administration resists, saying that public release of the memos would only hamstring their efforts to keep America safe. More troubling for them may be the comments from both inside and outside this country that their actions in killing a suspected terrorist, outside a declared war zone, might be illegal. I am certain that the administration feels (as I do) that its actions were justified. But if the administration is wise, it is giving some thought to the precedent it set itself. When a new administration comes to power, its well-intentioned actions may be judged in an entirely different light.

. . .

As they look over their shoulders dealing with the countless security challenges they face, officials in this administration and those that follow will be tempted to trim their actions with the goal of preventing controversy rather than preventing crisis. What courses of action they decide to take will long be debated. For me, it is all about leadership. It is easy for armchair quarterbacks, and politicians not in power, to simply say, "You must do the right thing." Figuring out what that thing is can be only half the problem. Then you must decide if you are willing to pay the price for being right.

One of the most essential factors for me was loyalty to the people I led. That loyalty was my moral compass. I could not operate any other way. I was strengthened by the knowledge that that loyalty worked both ways, and time and again my fidelity to my people was repaid manyfold by their incredible support for me.

When you make difficult decisions you must do so with the hope but not the expectation that in the end your actions will be validated and vindicated. The easiest thing in the world is to make no tough decisions. I could have had a much more placid and profitable life in recent years if I had elected to make no tough choices. Those who "go along to get along" rarely suffer negative consequences.

After years of investigation and scrutiny, I believe my actions were vindicated and, I must tell you, that judgment felt sweet. But there are no guarantees. A leader has choices to make. I chose to pursue hard measures. I have no regrets. I would do it all again, because it was the right thing to do—vindicated or not. I know our actions helped save American lives—and I can live with that.

AFTERWORD

Proving that there is no horse so dead that the bureaucracy can't work up the energy to beat it some more, my saga of the interrogation tapes did not end with word that the special prosecutor had decided not to prosecute me.

In November 2011, as I was finishing the manuscript for this book, I received the surprising news that John Durham had sent word to the CIA that while he could find no cause to bring me to trial, some sort of administrative action might be appropriate.

Deputy CIA Director Michael Morell, someone whom I worked closely with during my time at the Agency and whom I greatly respect, called me early one morning to inform me that Durham had suggested that the Agency consider whether I should receive a letter of reprimand for "insubordination." "I cannot hide my disappointment with the fact that after a three-year criminal investigation I continue to be hounded by my own government," I told him. "Nevertheless, if you can get former director Porter Goss or his boss, President George W. Bush, to say that I was insubordinate, I will take the rap."

This was not my first rodeo. I inquired about what the process would be. Because I was so senior at the time of my retirement, I was told, it would not be appropriate for more junior personnel to sit in judgment of my actions. The Agency considered several formulations for structuring an accountability board, but in the end it turned out to be a one-man board: Morell.

Subsequently, I met privately with Morell on one occasion and we talked about the tape saga. I appreciated his thorough knowledge of the record and his willingness to avoid a pro-longed process and make a quick decision.

On December 20, 2011, I was invited to come in to CIA headquarters to hear the verdict. Morell warmly welcomed me to his seventh-floor office and regretfully let me know his deci-sion. He essentially agreed with my assessment that you cannot be insubordinate to people outside your chain of command and, without directly saying so, conceded my point that they would not be able to get Director Goss or President Bush to characterize my actions as insubordination.

Instead, Morell said, he had recommended to General Petraeus, the new CIA director, that I receive a letter of repri-mand for failing to give the system "one more chance" to do the right thing. He said I knew, or should have known, that some people in government were uncomfortable with pro-ceeding with the destruction of the tapes. "Who?" I asked. He said among them was the vice president's chief of staff. At that moment I couldn't even remember who that had been. Morell reminded me it was David Addington. But I have no recollec-tion of ever hearing such a view from him. Mike said he found some reference to Addington's position by reading files. He also said that the president's counsel, Harriet Miers, and Director of National Intelligence John Negroponte, had expressed con-cern—and he was sure I knew about them because he had just read the chapter on the tapes from the draft of this memoir, which I had dutifully submitted to the CIA for clearance. I told him that I never heard anything directly from either of them but had eventually heard that they were among those who held the view that the time wasn't ripe to get rid of the tapes.

However, I viewed those expressions as opinions and not direct orders. Since I was told by Agency lawyers I was within my rights to act—I did.

Nonetheless, Morell said they had decided to give me the letter. He handed me a copy with classification markings on it—meaning I would not even be able to keep a copy. I was asked to sign the letter, which I did with the understanding that my signature indicated only that I had seen the letter, not that I agreed with it.

I asked what the next steps would be. Morell told me that the Agency was obliged to brief the White House about it but that he did not believe it was an issue that was of much interest to them. He said the House and Senate Intelligence Oversight Committees would also be briefed. It was my view, I told him, that the existence of the reprimand would leak from one of those two bodies.

The practical implication of the letter is nil. But in my view the letter and the entire process are an embarrassment—to the Agency, not to me. CIA officers who were in harm's way first asked the CIA to deal with a threat to their safety presented by the tapes in August 2002. More than three years later, after endless hand-wringing, dithering, and stalling on the part of the bureaucracy, I made a decision to act to protect my people. A three-year criminal investigation that followed showed that there was no legal impediment to my doing so. To say that I should have given the bureaucracy "one last chance" is incongruous. If I had done so, we would still be waiting for the system to make up its mind. If the Agency ever declassifies my letter of reprimand and gives me a copy, I'll have it framed. To me it says: Courage to Act.

ACKNOWLEDGMENTS

Words cannot describe the sense of amazement that I felt when I first walked into the imposing lobby of the Central Intelligence Agency's headquarters building as a new employee in November 1976. The enormous Agency seal on the marble floor, the stars of the fallen heroes on the wall, the grand statue of the father of American intelligence, General Donovan, sent chills down my spine as I reflected on the legacy and mystique of the organization I had just joined. I was filled with a mixture of excitement and anxiety as I contemplated the challenge of a career as a clandestine intelligence officer for the United States of America.

I retired thirty-one years later after a fabulous career that took me from a career trainee to the head of the National Clandestine Service. During those thirty-one years I had the good fortune to work with some of the most dedicated, patriotic, bright, and capable public servants in the U.S. government. As I climbed the ranks of my Agency, I learned much about leadership from two early supervisors. Jim Adkins taught me by example to protect the people who worked for me and not be afraid of doing the right thing even if it defied conventional wisdom. Jack McCavitt protected me and others who worked for him from the imbroglio of Iran-Contra. He also taught me not to take myself too seriously and to inject humor into everyday life. There were others who were running the Latin America Division in the mideighties and early nineties who taught me the craft of clandestine human operations and who served as mentors and advisors as I assumed positions of increasing responsibility. For fear of leaving someone out, I want to express my gratitude to them as a group.

I want to thank those who worked most closely with me during the last ten years of my career. Since many of them cannot have their full names revealed publicly, I choose to identify them all by first names only. My gratitude goes out to special assistants Libby, Peggy, Assunta, and Donna. As gatekeepers to my office they reflected the sense of openness, friendliness, and accessibility that I wanted to convey to all who called. A very special thanks to my chief of staff and loyal friend "Jane." She endured intense scrutiny by federal agents and the special prosecutor because of her close working relationship with me. I will forever be grateful to her for her wise counsel and dedicated service. I thank "Sara" for her brilliant work and immense contribution in CTC and as a component chief in the NCS. I am grateful to my favorite rapper, Anne Marie, and to all my executive assistants who got up so early and worked so hard to support me. I thank Ric, Paco, and Fernando for their friendship and loyal service. We shared very special times together.

I was fortunate to work with many excellent deputies both overseas and at headquarters. I thank Clay, Marilyn, Linda, Pat, Gerry, Bill, Tom, Bruce, Phil, Rob, John, and Hendrik. A special thanks to Terry, Jed, Bob, and Cindy.

Over the years there were proposals from Congress and outside experts to extract the clandestine service from the CIA to create a stand-alone human intelligence organization. I opposed those proposals because I believed the clandestine service needed the other three Agency directorates to do its mission. The Agency has the best analysts in the world. I worked closely with many of them over the years and respect their work and their important contribution to the intelligence mission. We have the brightest scientists and technologists in the intelligence community. They give the NCS that added edge that allows it to be the premier human intelligence service in the world. Our support personnel in the Directorate of Support never get the recognition they deserve. Whether serving side by side with the operators in the field or supporting us from headquarters, they are indispensable.

I thank the OGC lawyers who were assigned to my office in the Counterterrorism Center and in the NCS. I am sorry for the difficulty that my decisions have created for you.

I worked closely with three Agency directors. I thank George Tenet for giving me the opportunity to lead the Counterterrorism Center and for his leadership in the days, months, and years after 9/11. I am grateful to Porter Goss for his support and friendship during my tenure as head of the clandestine service and his defense of our mission and our officers. I will forever be thankful to General Mike Hayden for his personal support of me during the tapes investigation. My decision to destroy the tapes was made before he became director, and he could have easily punted. Instead, he not only supported my actions, he became a lonely but articulate and vocal defender of the Agency's interrogation programs. Thank you, Mike, for being a stand-up guy!

I had the opportunity to work closely with four other outstanding military officers who were assigned to the CIA after 9/11. They were Vice Admiral Bert Calland, USN, Ret., Lieutenant General John "Soup" Campbell, USAF, Ret., Major General Mike Ennis, USMC, Ret., and Brigadier General Mike Jones, USA, Ret. The CIA has never worked more closely with the U.S. military than in the past ten years, and these officers brought us closer together. They are also the type of guys I would like to share a beer with anytime, anywhere. Thank you, gentlemen!

I worked closely with the U.S. intelligence and law enforcement communities at home and abroad and always appreciated their valuable collaboration. I want to thank in particular retired FBI agents Luis Fernandez and Raul Roldan.

I had the good fortune to work with excellent U.S ambassadors during my seven overseas tours of duty. In particular, I am grateful to Ambassadors Dean Hinton, Ed Corr, and Jeff Davidow for their leadership and their wisdom.

I thank my successor as director of the National Clandestine Service, Mike Sulick, for his strong support for me during the special prosecutor's three-year investigation. I also thank Jim Pavitt, John Bennett, Dave Carey, Mike Morell, John McLaughlin, and Buzzy Krongard. A special recognition to our departed colleague and friend Ben Bonk, one of the gentlest and most decent human beings I ever knew. We also cherish the memories of our departed colleagues Les and Jonathan.

My employment prospects following retirement in 2008 were adversely affected by all the media hype surrounding the tapes issue. I want to thank Jeremy King from Benchmark Executive Search for helping me. I am thankful to my friends and colleagues in the private sector Andy, Frank, Chris, and Armand for taking a chance on me. I thank them for their patience in bringing me in from the cold and introducing me to a new and interesting world.

I thank my collaborator, Bill Harlow, for taking my story and turning it into an interesting and compelling book. I always marveled at the ease and speed with which Bill took my words and turned them into clear and readable prose. When I first approached Bill about helping me with this book I did not realize what a partnership it would become and how much trust and confidence in each other it would require. We have become very close as a result and I am grateful for his contribution and for his friendship.

Bill and I interviewed dozens of my former colleagues to check my recollections of events portrayed in this book and to hear the other side of the story from people who shared with me many of the important moments depicted here. I am deeply indebted to all of them, but for reasons they will understand, it is best not to identify them, even by first name.

As a former CIA officer, I have a lifetime obligation to submit anything I write to the Agency's Publication Review Board (PRB) to protect legitimately classified material and intelligence sources and methods. The manuscript for this book was submitted as required. The PRB did not authorize me to include everything I would have liked. For example, a lengthy section on a sensitive but widely misunderstood and mischaracterized program was removed at their insistence. Additionally, I agreed to modify a few facts, figures, and details in order to protect Agency programs, officers, and those who worked with the CIA. In virtually every instance, if I had been permitted to be more precise, the case I make in the book about the value and necessity of Agency actions would only have been strengthened. Nonetheless, I understand and support the work of the PRB and thank its members for their very thorough, aggressive, and appropriate efforts to protect necessary secrets. I appreciate their professionalism and willingness to work with me to help ensure I could tell this story as fully as possible. I want to point out that with the exception of very well-known public figures, such as former CIA directors, U.S. senators, and the like, I have tried to avoid using the true names of CIA officers. In some cases I use pseudonyms, which are in quotes at the first use.

My lawyer, Bob Bennett, came into my life as if by divine intervention at a time when the Congress, the Department of Justice, and the media were coming after me. Knowing that I had a world-class litigator representing me brought peace of mind during very trying times. Over the years Patti and I got to know and share time with Bob and his lovely wife, Ellen, and consider them to be our very special friends. I also want to thank Bob's partner, Carl Rauh, and Bob's special assistant, Judy Sachs.

Over the course of my career, I have worked with many agents, but never before with one of the literary kind. I was blessed to have one of the best in the business, Andrew Wylie. I thank Andrew and his former deputy, Scott Moyers, for easing my initiation into the publishing world.

Louise Burke, executive vice president and publisher at Simon & Schuster, was among the first to recognize the importance of writing *Hard Measures,* and she assigned some of her best people to help us. I want to thank Mitchell Ivers of Simon & Schuster, whose enthusiasm for this project never wavered from the first day we met and whose skill and advice as an editor made it infinitely better. We are grateful to Jennifer Robinson and Mary McCue for aggressively employing their publicity skills to help make sure the reading public was aware of this book.

Patti and I have the good fortune of having many friends around the world who support us and love us no matter what. I want to single out our dear friends Barb and Rick and their daughters, Megan and Carly. I also thank our friends Don and Sherry, Don and Carolyn, Guillermo and Serpa, Wayne and Carla, Chris and Rosslyn, Barry and Rosana, and Peg and David. A special thanks to my biggest fans and supporters and longtime family friends from Cape Cod—Doris, Carl, and Mary.

My parents, Jose Angel and Lucy, knitted the fabric of my character and molded me into the person I am today. They gave me a value system rooted in honesty, trustworthiness, loyalty, and fairness. The hardest decisions I made as a leader in the clandestine service reflected the value system and moral compass of my upbringing. I owe them everything.

My brother, Willie, sister, Ivelisse, their spouses, Doris and David, and their children, Melissa, Natalia, Daniel, and grandson Alejandro were a source of love and support during the trials and tribulations of the past few years.

My mother-in-law, Jean, prayed hard and lit many candles for me. My father-in-law, Ed "Fatty," died suddenly twenty years ago, but I know he was pulling for us from up above. I am grateful to my sister-in-law, Jan, her husband, Mike, and their children, Kyle, Cara, and her husband, Mike, for their unwavering confidence in me.

I love my sons, Nic and Alec, more than they will ever know. They have grown into decent, respectful, kind, and sensitive human beings and I am very proud of them. This book is my legacy to them.

And then there is my beloved wife, Patti, my soul mate and best friend for the past thirty years. I met her on my first foreign assignment and married her before my second. Together we lived in six different countries, endured fifteen pack-outs, hosted hundreds of invited guests to our homes, and attended an even greater number of diplomatic dinners and receptions. We had a lot of fun during our seventeen years overseas and made many friends, but we also had to deal with crime, danger, natural disasters, and disease. As I ascended the ranks in my career she shared my greatest accomplishments as well as my deepest disappointments. While I worked twelve- to fourteen-hour days she worked even longer days caring for our children, running the household, and working outside the home whenever the opportunity presented itself. I could not have had the career I had without her love and support. My love for her grows with each passing day.